W9-CDO-006

ECONOMICS
IN WONDERLAND

Senior Editor: J. MICHAEL CATRON
Supervising Editor: GARY GROTH
Designers: JACOB COVEY and KEELI McCARTHY
Editorial Assistants: R.J. CASEY, CONRAD GROTH
Production: PRESTON WHITE
Associate Publisher: ERIC REYNOLDS
Publisher: GARY GROTH

Fantagraphics Books, Inc.
7563 Lake City Way NE
Seattle, WA 98115
(800) 657-1100
Fantagraphics.com. • Twitter: @fantagraphics • facebook.com/fantagraphics.

First Fantagraphics Books edition: November 2017
ISBN 978-1-68396-060-7
Library of Congress Control Number: 2017938237
Printed in China

Robert B. REICH

A CARTOON GUIDE TO A POLITICAL WORLD GONE MAD AND MEAN

ECONOMICS IN WONDERLAND

FANTAGRAPHICS BOOKS

CONTENTS

TRUMPONOMICS

INTRODUCTION

Several years ago, my son Sam, a film producer and director, gave me some frank advice. "I know you like to write books," Sam said. "And books are important. But my generation is especially receptive to film and video. Have you thought about a different medium for your ideas?"

I hadn't. But I was open to it.

I had written a number of books that charted America's economic and political problems: stagnant wages, widening inequality, and the angers and frustrations that both produce, ultimately resulting in widespread rejection of the political status quo.

But I was receptive to Sam's suggestion. I had taught two generations of college students, and I had noticed a subtle but unmistakable change in the way they absorbed information and analysis.

A few months after Sam spoke with me, a young film director named Jacob Kornbluth met me in my office at the University of California Berkeley with a proposition that fit perfectly with Sam's suggestion.

Jake wanted to do a film based on my recent book, *Aftershock*, about how the financial crisis of 2008 had opened people's eyes to gaping inequalities of income, wealth, and political power.

I had no idea how Jake could go about making the film. "These are complex ideas," I told him. "They don't lend themselves to film."

Jake reassured me there'd be no problem.

Over the next two years, Jake and his team produced *Inequality for All*, a documentary that went on to win a Special Jury Award at the Sundance Film Festival and appear in hundreds of theaters and on streaming video. The film continues to be viewed by college and high school students in classes on economics and politics.

Jake and I also started making short, two- or three-minute videos, explaining public policy issues that many people were confused about — ranging from President Obama's Affordable Care Act to Donald Trump's infrastructure plan.

I always loved to draw, and the videos Jake and I began doing gave me an opportunity to stand at an easel and sketch the ideas I was talking about in the videos.

People seemed to like the drawings and the videos. They told us the combination helped them understand better what was going on around them. To date, our videos have been viewed hundreds of millions of times.

I've discovered that Sam was right. Films and short, snappy videos with drawings are a way to get through to people who find it easier to think visually. I've also discovered that many explanations and arguments don't really need lots of words. They can be made forcefully in pictures and a few words.

This book reflects some of those efforts.

In this era of presidential whoppers and "fake news," it's particularly important to convey the truth in ways that people can understand.

— ROBERT REICH

BIG MONEY

WHAT'S THE FED? HOW IT AFFECTS YOU

One of the most important agencies in Washington D.C. is the Federal Reserve — usually just called "the Fed" for short.

The Fed has a big say in whether you have a job and what happens to your pay. That's because they essentially decide how high interest rates are going to be.

Here's the way it works: The lower the rate, the easier it is to borrow. The easier it is to borrow, the more active the economy becomes.

That's because when interest rates are low, we're paying less to the banks and more for the things we need, which increases demand. That, in turn, increases demand for labor, which leads to more jobs. Lots of jobs and employers have to pay higher wages and offer better working conditions to attract the workers they need.

This is good for everyone, especially those at the bottom end of the jobs and wage ladder. In the late 1990s when the economy was moving at a fast clip, unemployment got down to 4%, and even people at the bottom got a raise.

On the other hand, when the Fed raises rates, borrowing becomes harder and more costly. We spend more on our debts and less on the things we need. So fewer jobs are created and there's little or no pressure to raise wages.

Now, if this were the whole story, the Fed would obviously keep interest rates at or near zero, where they've been since the Great Recession of 2008.

But the Fed is also supposed to prevent inflation — price increases that get out of control, which happens when too much demand chases too few products. That's what the Fed weighs — whether to push for more jobs and higher wages or whether to prevent inflation, regardless of the costs to working families.

The Fed's Open Market Committee makes that decision several times a year, and some

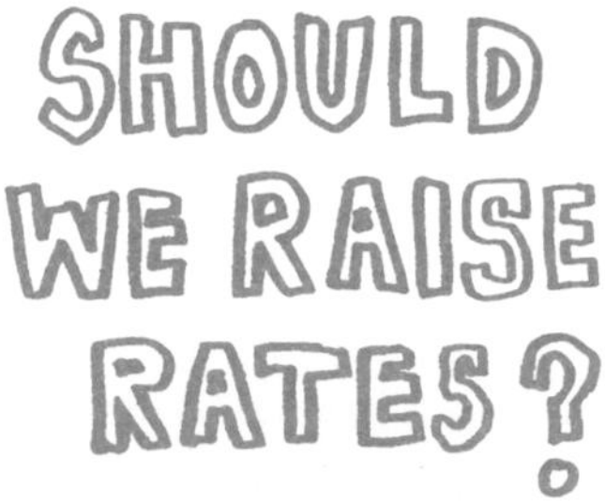
SHOULD WE RAISE RATES?

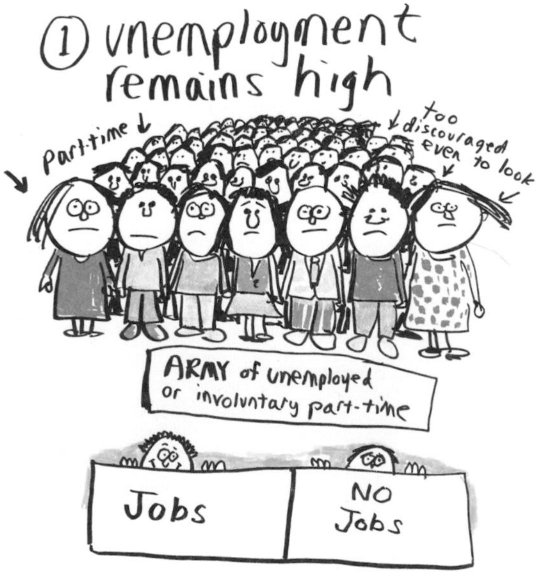
① unemployment remains high
part-time
too discouraged even to look
ARMY of unemployed or involuntary part-time
Jobs
NO Jobs

members are worried about inflation, so they're pushing to raise rates. But this would be a big mistake for three big reasons:

1) UNEMPLOYMENT REMAINS HIGH. when you factor in the millions of Americans who are still working part-time who would rather be working full-time and the millions of others who have stopped looking for work altogether because they haven't found any for years. These people have already been counted as unemployed. The percent of working-age Americans who have jobs is just about the lowest it has been in 35 years. If the Fed raises rates now, all this would get worse.

2) WAGES ARE STILL STUCK IN THE MUD. Median household income is 6% below what it was before the Great Recession. If the Fed raises rates, there's no chance for most people to get a wage increase. These trends hurt people of color and women the most. In 2014, the unemployment rate for blacks was 11.3%, more than double the white rate. And of course, women continue to make less than men for doing the same work.

When the economy is booming and employers are looking to hire more workers, it's harder for them to discriminate against black people and women. So those racial and gender gaps have the chance to shrink. But if the Fed raises rates, it will allow those disparities to get worse.

3) THERE'S NO SIGN OF INFLATION ANYWHERE. Overall prices are tame and where they're not, as with airlines and internet services, it's because companies don't have enough competition. Those companies can raise prices without fear that consumers will go elsewhere — not because demand is getting out of control.

Besides, inflation isn't like a genie that gets out of a bottle. If and when inflation breaks out, it can be contained by raising interest rates then. §

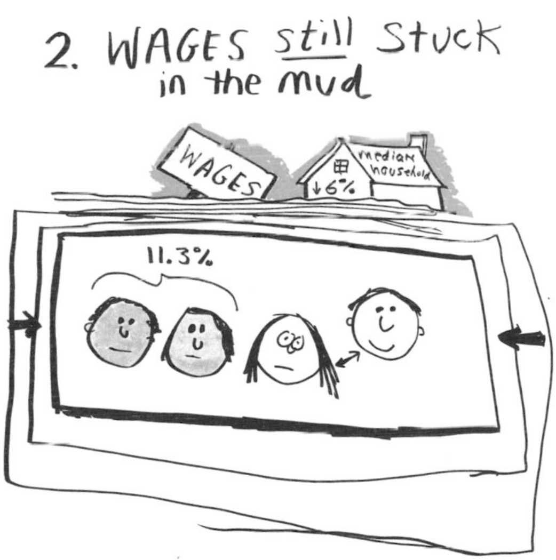
2. WAGES still stuck in the mud
WAGES
median household
↓6%
11.3%

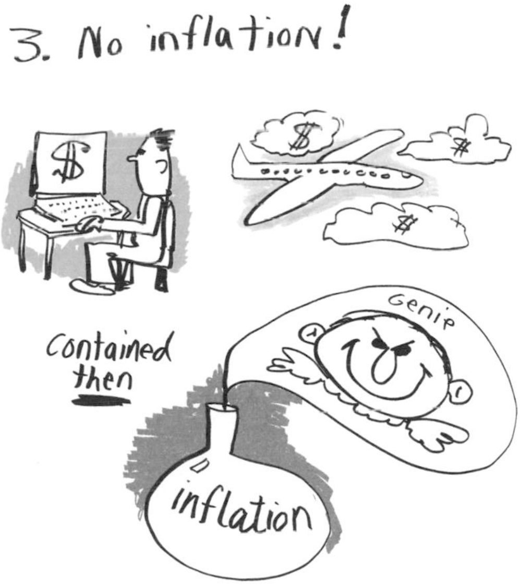
3. No inflation!
$
Genie
Contained then
inflation

SAVING CAPITALISM FOR THE MANY, NOT THE FEW

One of the most dangerously deceptive ideas is that the free market is natural and neutral.

The traditional economic debate imagines two parts to our economy: a private sector — the free market — and a public sector — the government. In this cartoon version, the free market pays people and distributes goods and services in a natural or neutral way. And government intrudes on the market by regulating the services, taxing some of what businesses and individuals earn, and then redistributing it.

Much of what conservatives and liberals debate is how much government intrusion into the so-called free market is acceptable to achieve an economy that works for most of us.

But this cartoon version leaves out a critical point. There is no free market in nature. The free market is really a set of rules created and enforced

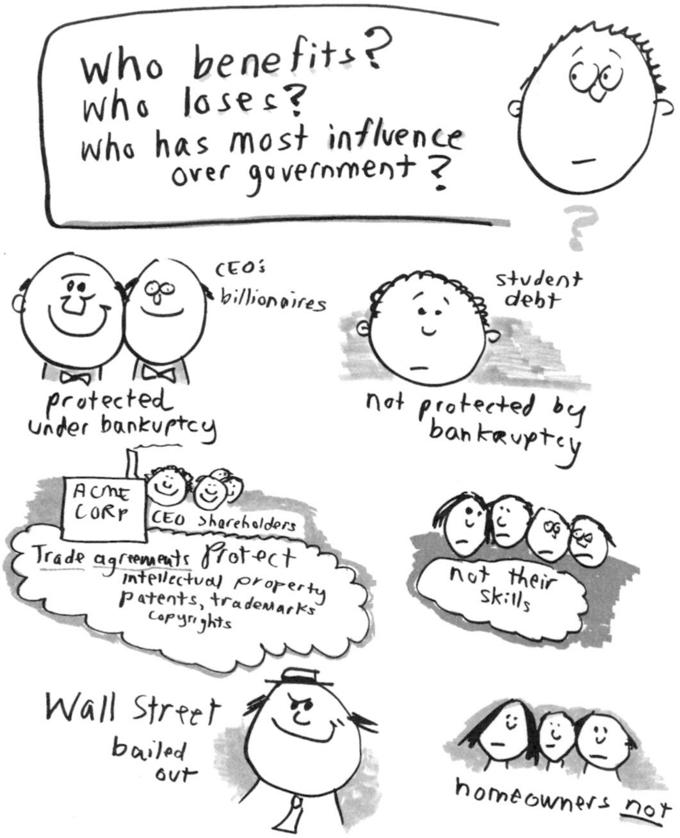

Who benefits?
Who loses?
Who has most influence over government?
CEO's billionaires
protected under bankruptcy
student debt
not protected by bankruptcy
ACME CORP
CEO shareholders
Trade agreements protect intellectual property patents, trademarks copyrights
not their skills
Wall Street
bailed out
homeowners not

by government. Elected officials, agency heads, and judges make the rules — and sometimes they change them. They create the market. The real issue is who the rules benefit, who they hurt, and who has the most influence over making them.

For example, the market provides bankruptcy protection for big corporations and billionaires, allowing them to shed their debts — including labor contracts. But it provides no bankruptcy protection for college graduates overburdened with student debt.

International trade agreements protect the intellectual property of large corporations, but they don't protect the accumulated skills of American workers.

Big Wall Street banks and their executives are bailed out when they can't pay what they owe, but not homeowners who can't meet their mort-

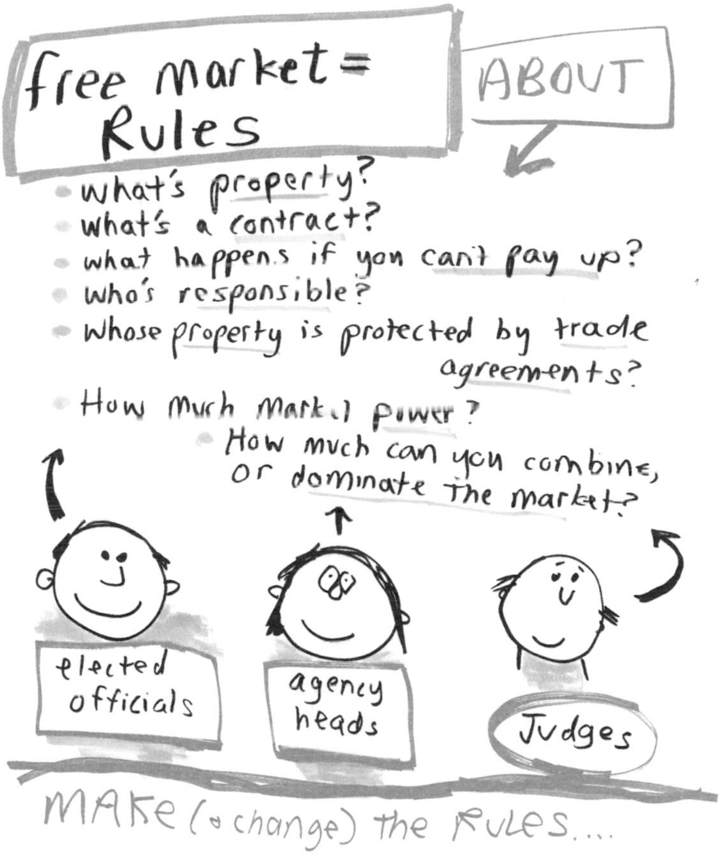
free market = Rules
ABOUT
what's property?
what's a contract?
what happens if you can't pay up?
who's responsible?
Whose property is protected by trade agreements?
How much market power?
How much can you combine, or dominate the market?
elected officials
agency heads
Judges
MAKE (or change) the RULES...

gage payments. American industries are allowed to consolidate into huge near-monopolies: big cable, big pharma, major airlines, health insurers, Wall Street banks, big agriculture, giant retailers.

But workers who want to join together in trade unions face all sorts of obstacles. They're fired with impunity as more states adopt so called "right-to-work laws" that undermine unions. These are just some of the rules of the so-called "free market."

If our democracy were working as it should, rules of the market would help most of us. Instead, as income and wealth has been concentrated at the top over the last 40 years, so has the power to

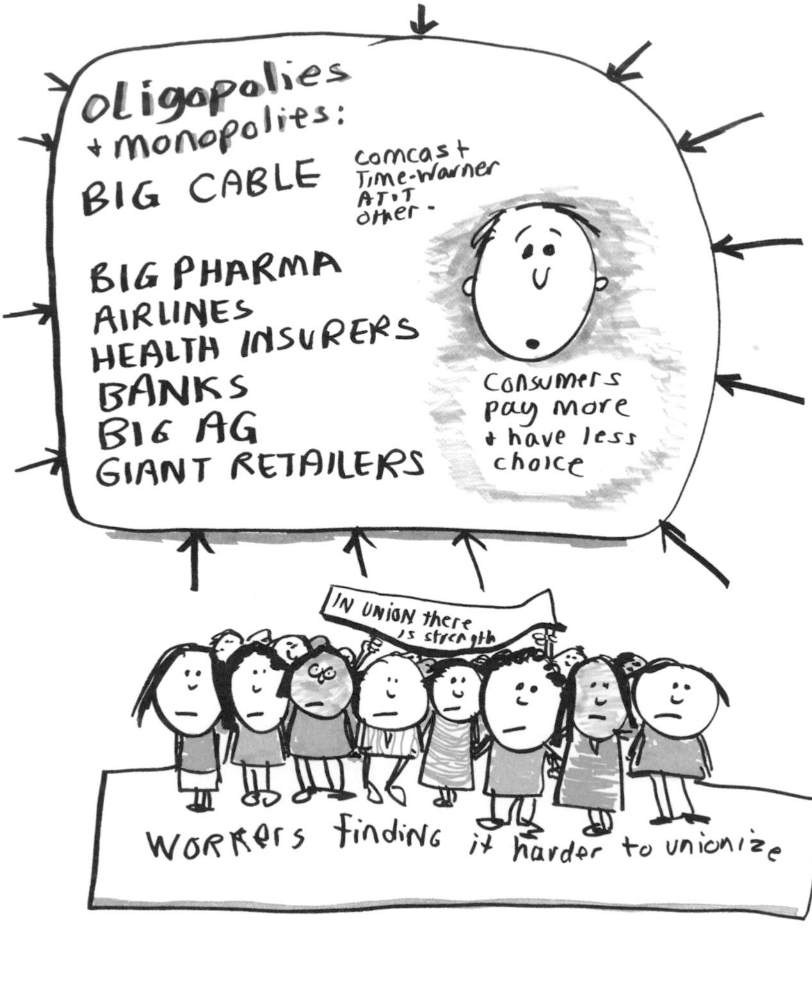

oligopolies + monopolies:
BIG CABLE
comcast Time-Warner AT+T other-
BIG PHARMA
AIRLINES
HEALTH INSURERS
BANKS
BIG AG
GIANT RETAILERS
consumers pay more + have less choice
IN UNION there is strength
WORKERS finding it harder to unionize

make the rules of the market by influencing the politicians and regulatory heads (even the courts, and the lawyers who appear before them), with the result that the market is rigged for the benefit of the wealthy few.

If we really want to reduce the savage inequalities and insecurities most people are experiencing, we shouldn't be swayed by the myth of a neutral free market.

We must make the market work for all of us rather than for only a few at the top. And to do that, we must exert the citizen power that is supposed to be ours. §

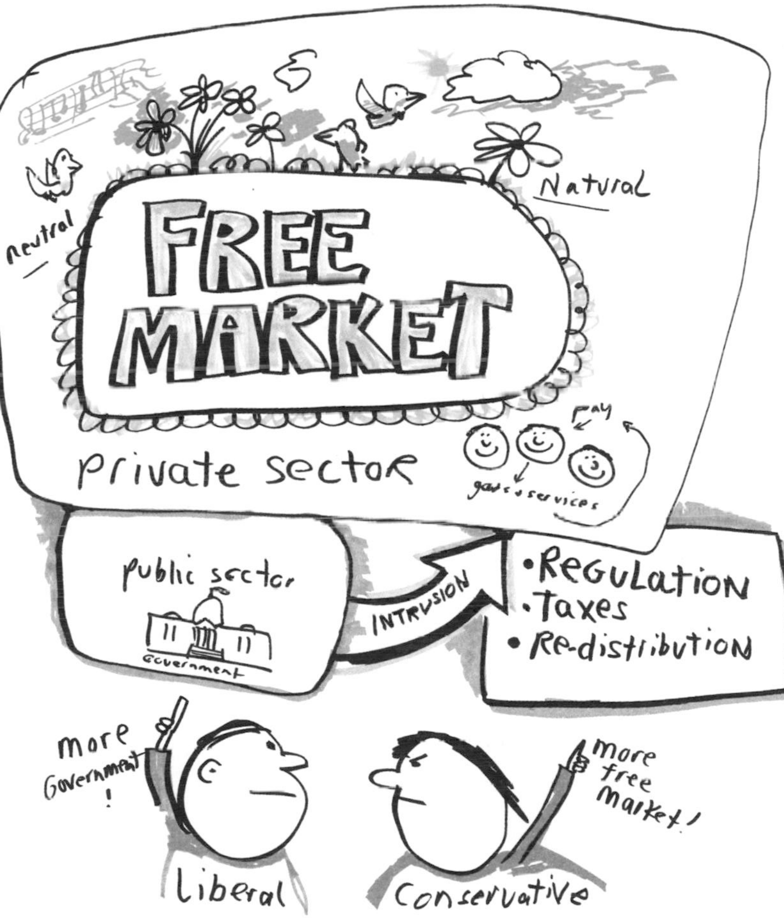
FREE MARKET
Natural
neutral
private sector
pay
goods & services
public sector
Government
INTRUSION
•Regulation
•Taxes
•Re-distibution
more Government!
more free market!
Liberal
Conservative

THE REALITY OF FREE TRADE DEALS

Most economists still think free trade benefits most Americans, but according to polls, only 35% of voters agree.

Why this discrepancy?

Because economists support any policy that improves efficiency, and they typically define a policy as efficient if the people who benefit from it *could* compensate those who lose from it and still come out ahead.

But this way of looking at things leaves out three big realities.

1) INEQUALITY KEEPS GROWING. In a society of widening inequality, the winners are often wealthier than the losers, so even if they fully compensate the losers, as the winners gain more ground, the losers may feel even worse off.

2) SAFETY NETS KEEP UNRAVELING. As a practical matter, the winners *don't* compensate the losers. Most of the losers from free trade — the millions whose good jobs have been lost — don't even have access to unemployment insurance.

Trade adjustment assistance is a joke. America invests less in job training as a percent of our economy than almost any other advanced nation.

3) MEDIAN PAY KEEPS DROPPING. Those whose paychecks have been declining because of free trade are not compensated for those declines by having access to cheaper goods and services from abroad. Yes, those cheaper goods help, but adjusted for inflation, the median hourly pay of production workers is still lower today than it was in 1974.

So if we want the public to support free trade, we must ensure that everyone benefits from it.

This means we need a genuine reemployment system — including not only *unemployment* insurance, but also *income* insurance. So if you lose your job and have to take one that pays less, you get a portion of the difference for up to a year.

More basically, we've got to ensure that the gains from free trade are more widely shared. §

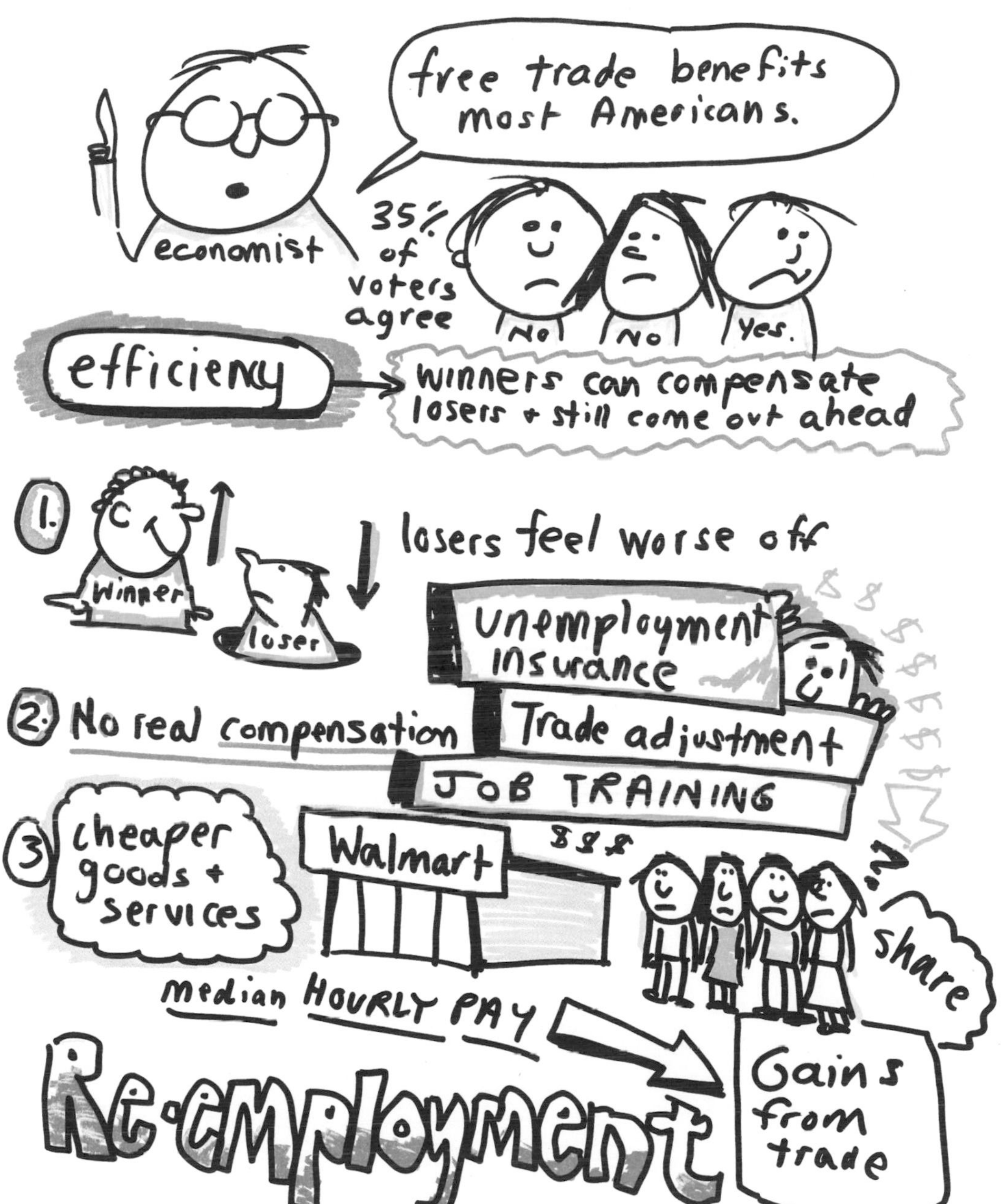
free trade benefits most Americans.
economist
35% of voters agree
No
No
Yes.
efficiency
winners can compensate losers + still come out ahead
1.
winner
loser
losers feel worse off
Unemployment insurance
2. No real compensation
Trade adjustment
JOB TRAINING
3 cheaper goods + services
Walmart
share
median HOURLY PAY
Re-employment
Gains from trade

PUTTING A LID ON TAX EXPENDITURES

The federal government currently diverts hundreds of billions of tax dollars every year to help the wealthiest Americans become even wealthier. How? Through so-called tax expenditures — the equivalent of government handouts, that allow the wealthy to deduct or exclude from their taxable incomes large amounts of employer-provided healthcare, retirement savings, and mortgage interest. These three tax expenditures demand reform for three big reasons:

FIRST, THEY ARE UNFAIR. Middle- and low-income workers don't get from their employers nearly as much health insurance and retirement income as do corporate executives. Many get none at all. And their mortgages — if they have any — are usually much smaller, because they live in homes that don't cost as much.

SECOND, THESE DEDUCTIONS AND EXCLUSIONS ARE NONSENSICAL. Originally, they were put into the tax code to give people financial incentives to get health insurance, to save for retirement, and to buy a home. But the rich don't need incentives to do these things because they're … rich.

FINALLY, THESE THREE DEDUCTIONS AND EXCLUSIONS COST HUNDREDS OF BILLIONS OF DOLLARS A YEAR — $348 billion in 2015 alone — the lion's share going to high-income families. Instead of wasting these billions on making the wealthy even wealthier, we should be using these resources to provide better healthcare, retirement security, and affordable housing to low- and middle-income households, including households of color, who are currently losing out.

In sum, there's no reason why America's wealthy should be able to deduct or exclude from their taxable incomes more than, say, $25,000 a year for employer-provided healthcare, retirement, and mortgage interest.

Limiting those deductions and exclusions would be rational, fiscally responsible, and fair. §

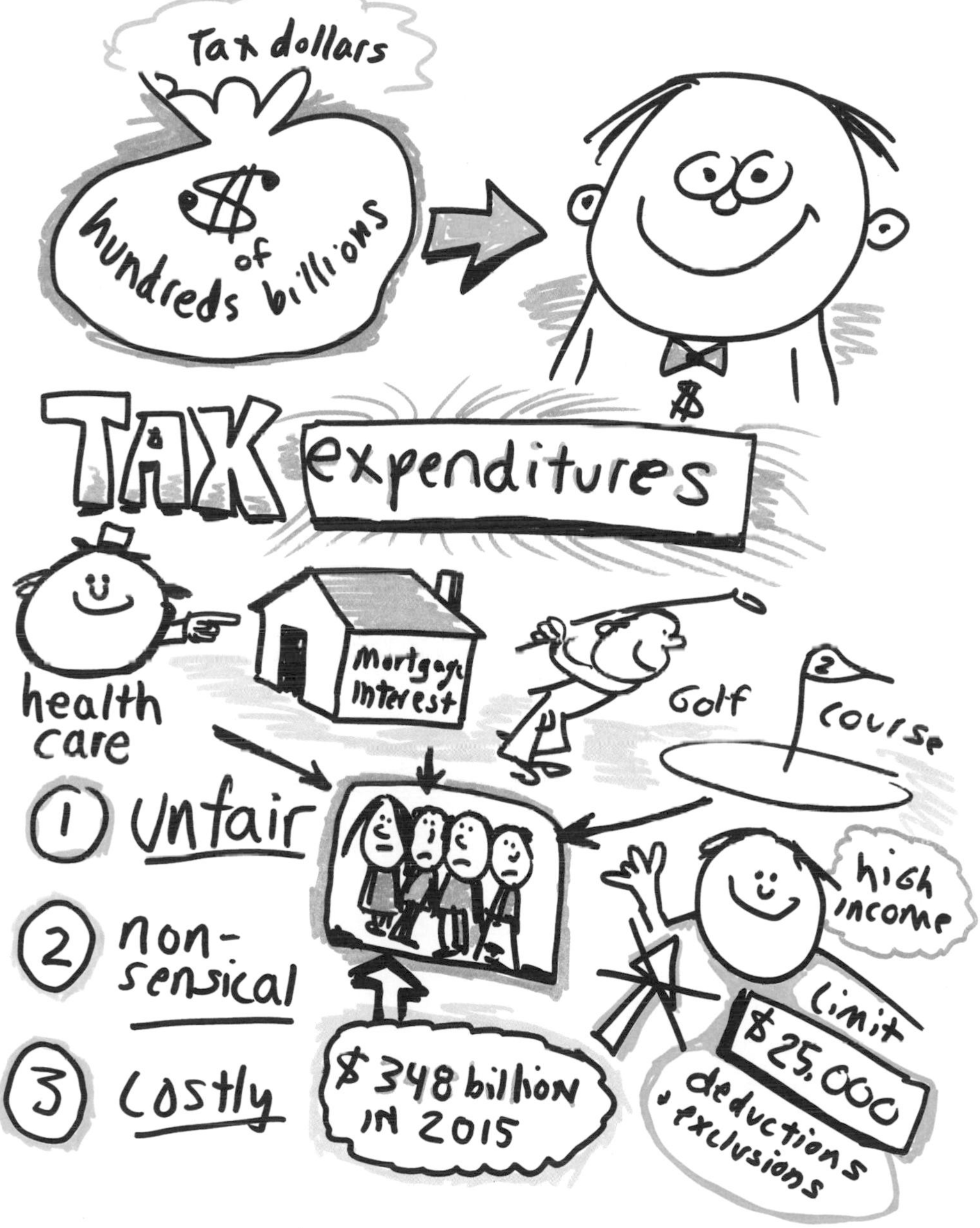
Tax dollars
hundreds of billions
$
TAX expenditures
health care
Mortgage interest
Golf course
high income
limit
$25,000
deductions & exclusions
1 Unfair
2 non-sensical
3 Costly
$348 billion in 2015

CORPORATE TAX DESERTION

Corporations are deserting America because they want lower taxes abroad. Some politicians say the only way to stop these desertions is to reduce corporate tax rates in the United States so they won't leave.

Wrong.

If we start trying to match lower corporate tax rates around the world, there will be no end to it. Instead, the president and the Treasury Department should use their executive power to end the financial incentives that encourage this type of desertion.

In addition, any corporation that deserts America should no longer be entitled to the advantages of being American.

1) THEY SHOULDN'T BE ALLOWED TO CONTRIBUTE TO U.S. POLITICAL CAMPAIGNS, or lobby Congress, or participate in U.S. government agency rulemaking proceedings. And they should no longer have the right to sue foreign companies in U.S. courts for acts committed outside of the United States.

2) THEY SHOULDN'T BE ENTITLED TO GENEROUS GOVERNMENT CONTRACTS. "Buy American" provisions of the law should be applied to them.

3) THEIR INTERNATIONAL ASSETS SHOULD NO LONGER BE PROTECTED BY THE U.S. GOVERNMENT. If their factories and equipment are expropriated somewhere around the world, they shouldn't expect the United States to negotiate or threaten sanctions. If their intellectual property, patents, trademarks, trade names, and copyrights are disregarded, that's their problem, too.

They don't get to be represented by the United States government because they are no longer American.

It's simple logic. If corporations want to desert America in order to pay less in taxes, that's their business — but they should no longer have the benefits that come with being American. §

Any corporation that deserts America should no longer be entitled to the advantages of being American.

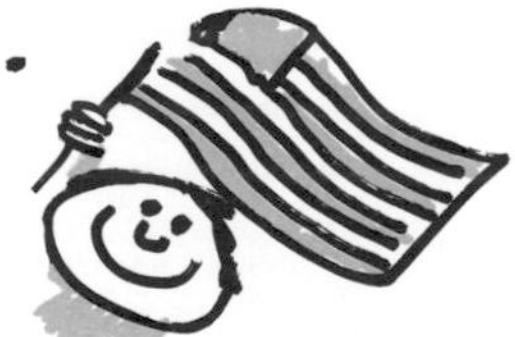

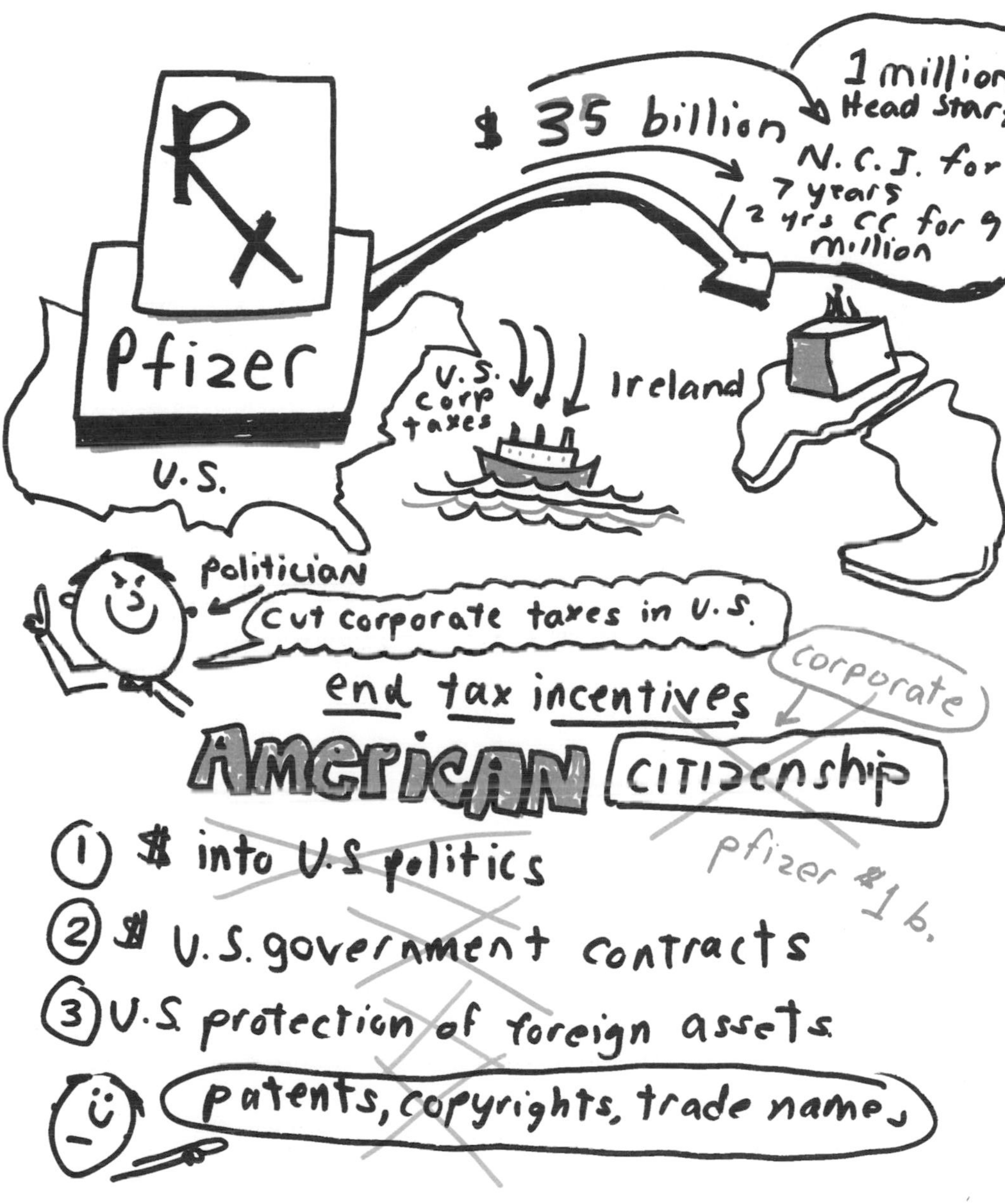

Pfizer
U.S.
$ 35 billion
1 million Head Start
N.C.J. for 7 years
2 yrs CC for 9 million
U.S. corp taxes
Ireland
politician
Cut corporate taxes in U.S.
end tax incentives
corporate
American citizenship
pfizer $1 b.
① $ into U.S politics
② $ U.S. government contracts
③ U.S protection of foreign assets.
patents, copyrights, trade names

POWER: WHO HAS IT, WHO DOESN'T

Whose power?

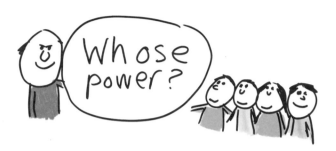

Power. These days, most Americans have little or none — not as employees, or consumers, or even voters. The companies we work for, the corporations and banks we deal with, and the political system we participate in have all been taken over by a relatively small group of very wealthy and privileged people.

It didn't used to be this way, and it doesn't have to continue. It's time to take the power back.

1) CONSIDER THE DECLINE OF WORKER POWER. 50 years ago, a third of private sector workers belonged to unions, which gave them the bargaining power to get a substantial share of the economy's gains. Now fewer than 7% are unionized, and most of the economy's gains go to the top.

CEOs who earned 20 times the pay of average workers in the 1960s are now hauling in 300 times their pay. Inequality is out of control. We need stronger unions, and workers need a louder voice.

2) ALONG WITH DECLINING WORKER POWER, CORPORATE AND FINANCIAL POWER HAS GROWN. Just over a century ago, Teddy Roosevelt — a Republican — busted up the Standard Oil Trust and other giant monopolies. In 1933, Franklin D. Roosevelt enacted the Glass-Steagall Act that separated investment from commercial banking.

Now, due to a combination of deregulation and greed that allowed the financial industry to run amok, a handful of giant banks have a chokehold

CEOs → 300x
1. WORKER POWER
economic gains
50 years ago
Now 7%
most gains
Stronger unions
louder voice

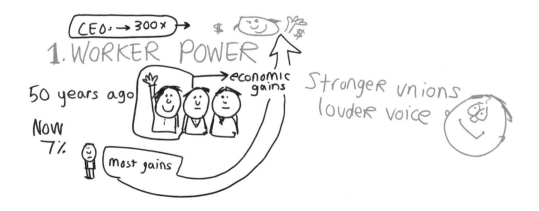

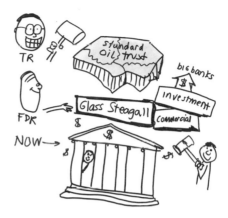

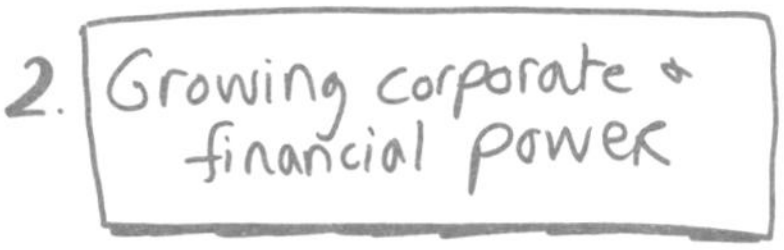

2. Growing corporate & financial power

TR
standard oil trust
big banks
investment
FDR
Glass Steagall
commercial
NOW

on the entire economy — and we're heading for another "too big to fail" financial crisis.

We must institute stronger protections for the economy — and for all of us — such as resurrecting Glass-Steagall and busting up the biggest banks.

3) **BIG MONEY HAS TAKEN OVER OUR DEMOCRACY.** The moneyed interests have driven down corporate tax rates and expanded income tax loopholes. During the administration of Republican president Dwight D. Eisenhower, the super-rich paid a marginal tax rate of over 90%. Now, the highest tax rate is less than half that, and — because of countless tax loopholes — most of the wealthy pay far less than 30%, a rate that is lower than many middle-class families pay.

We need higher taxes on the wealthy to do what needs to be done for the nation — like free public higher education. And we must get Big Money out of politics. §

3.
BIG MONEY
American democracy?
Lower corporate taxes
more tax loopholes

Republican
Dwight Eisenhower
over 90%
top marginal rate
NOW ↓ 30%

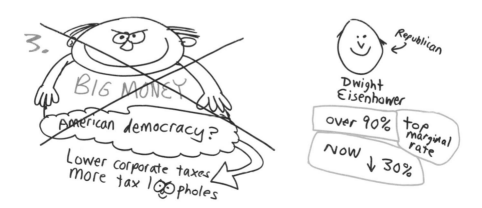

THE INVESTMENTS OF THE 158

According to an investigation by *The New York Times*, half of all the money contributed to the Democratic and Republican presidential candidates by October of 2015 — $176 million — had come from just 158 families, along with the companies they own or control.

Who are these people? They're almost entirely white, older, male, and rich — even though America is becoming increasingly black and brown, young, female, and with declining household incomes.

According to the report, most of these big contributors live in exclusive neighborhoods where they have private security guards instead of public police officers and private health facilities rather than public parks and pools.

Most send their kids and grandkids to elite private schools rather than public schools. They fly in private jets and get driven in private limousines rather than rely on public transportation.

They don't have to worry about whether Social Security or Medicare will be there for them in their retirement because they have put away huge fortunes. They don't have to worry about climate change because they don't live in flimsy homes that might collapse in a hurricane or where water is scarce or their food supply is endangered.

It's doubtful that most of these 158 are contributing to these campaigns out of the goodness of their hearts or a sense of public responsibility. They're largely making investments, just the way they make other investments.

And the success of these investments depends on whether their candidates get elected — to lower their taxes even more; expand tax loopholes; shred health, safety, and environmental regulations so their companies can make even more money; cut Social Security, Medicare, and programs for the poor — and thereby allow these 158 and others like them to secede even farther from the rest of our society.

These people, after all, do live in their own separate society, and they want to elect people who represent them, not the rest of us.

How much more evidence do we need that the American system is in crisis? How long before we make that system work for all of us instead of a handful at the top?

We must not let them buy our democracy. We must get big money out of politics, publicly finance political campaigns, require disclosure of all sources of campaign funds — and reverse the Supreme Court's *Citizens United* decision. §

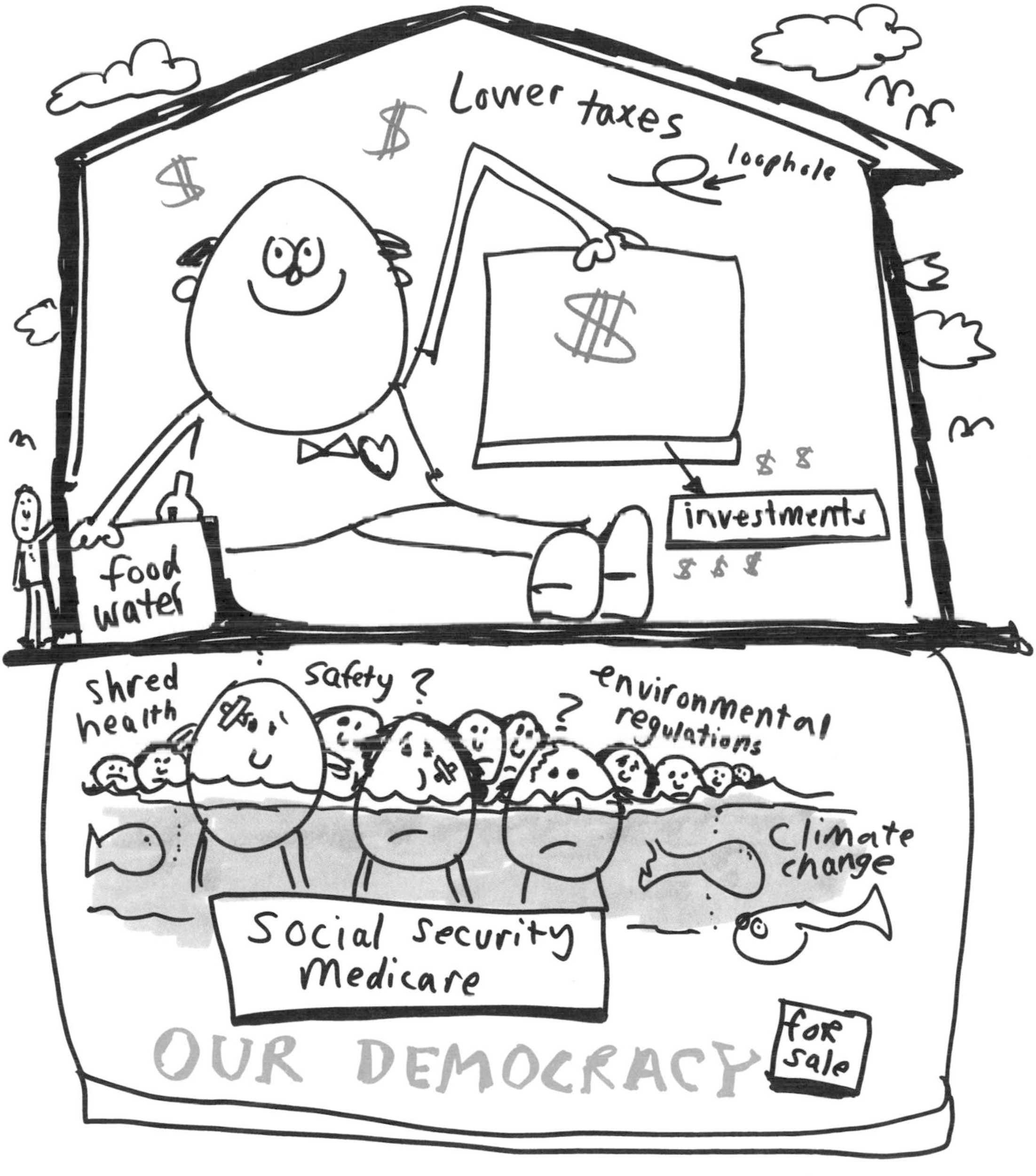
Lower taxes
loophole
investments
food
water
shred health
safety ?
environmental regulations
Climate change
Social security
Medicare
OUR DEMOCRACY
for sale

WHY THE KOCH MACHINE
IS A THREAT TO DEMOCRACY

A number of billionaires are flooding our democracy with their money, drowning out the voices of the rest of us. But Charles and David Koch are in a class by themselves. They're using their fortune (they're the fifth and sixth richest people in the world) to create their own political machine, designed to protect and advance their financial interests.

The Koch machine includes:

1) POLITICAL FRONT GROUPS pouring hundreds of millions of dollars into elections at every level of our democracy while disguising the sources of the money.

2) GIANT ADVERTISING CAMPAIGNS to convince Americans climate change is a myth, the Affordable Care Act will harm them, unions are bad, and wealthy people deserve tax cuts.

3) A NETWORK OF THINK TANKS designed to come up with findings that the Kochs want. For example, millions of dollars for studies arguing we should abolish the minimum wage or keep it where it is forever.

4) A CAMPAIGN TO SUPPRESS THE VOTES of minorities. Funding white poll watchers where minorities vote — leading to complaints of voter intimidation — and peddling a "Voter ID Bill" to state legislatures across the country designed to make it harder for many to vote.

5) A NATIONWIDE EFFORT TO BUST UNIONS, funding anti-union campaigns in states like Wisconsin and pushing an anti-union law that's been used in dozens of states to undermine workers' collective bargaining rights.

6) A LONG-TERM STRATEGY TO UNRAVEL AMERICA'S CAMPAIGN FINANCE LAWS, even organizing secret meetings with sympathetic Supreme Court Justices.

The Koch political machine would be troubling in any circumstance, but it's especially dangerous in present-day America where wealth is more concentrated than it's been in over a century. And the Supreme Court has opened the floodgates to big money.

The problem is not that the Kochs are so rich or that their political views are so regressive. The problem is that they're using their exorbitant wealth to impose those views on the rest of us, undermining our democracy. §

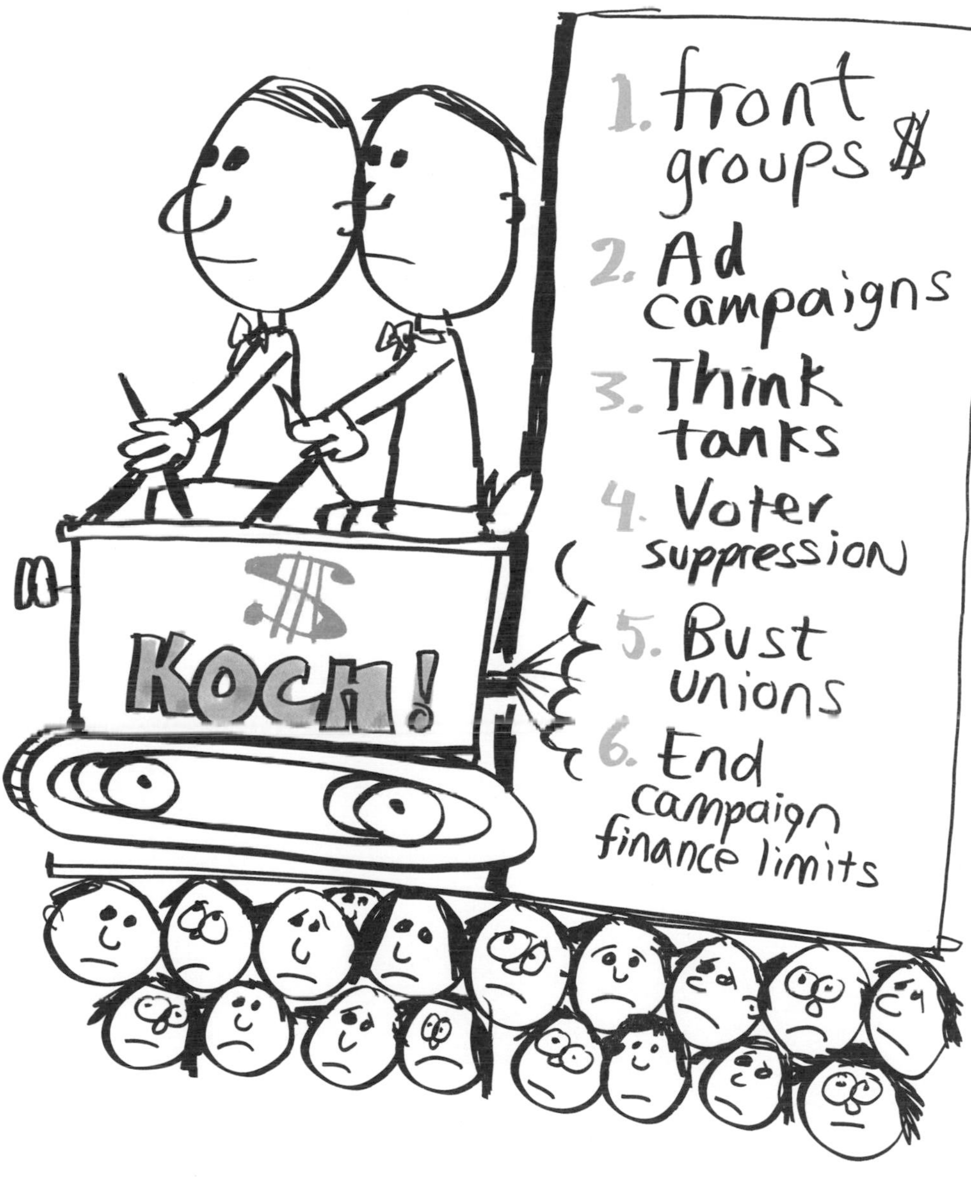
1. front groups $
2. Ad campaigns
3. Think tanks
4. Voter suppression
5. Bust unions
6. End campaign finance limits
KOCH!

SHAMS, SCAMS,
AND FLIM-FLAMS

PAUL RYAN'S SEVEN TERRIBLE IDEAS

Speaker of the House of Representatives Paul Ryan is the man in charge of delivering on Republican campaign promises.

Keep a wary eye out for Speaker Ryan's seven favorite ideas:

1) REDUCE THE TOP INCOME TAX RATE TO 25% — or less — from the current 39%. A terrible idea. That would create a huge windfall for the rich at a time when they already take home a larger share of total U.S. income than at any time since the 1920s.

2) CUT CORPORATE TAXES TO 25% — or less — from the current 35%. Another bad idea. This one is a giant sop to corporations, the largest of which are already socking away trillions of dollars in foreign tax shelters.

3) SLASH SPENDING ON DOMESTIC PROGRAMS like food stamps and education for poor districts. Already, 22% of the nation's children live in poverty. These cuts would only make things worse.

4) TURN MEDICAID AND OTHER FEDERAL PROGRAMS FOR THE POOR INTO BLOCK GRANTS for the states, and then let the states decide how to allocate them. In other words, give Republican state legislatures and governors slush funds to do with as they please.

5) TURN MEDICARE INTO VOUCHERS THAT DON'T KEEP UP WITH INCREASES IN HEALTHCARE COSTS. In effect, cut Medicare for the elderly. Another awful Ryan idea.

6) RAISE THE RETIREMENT AGE FOR SOCIAL SECURITY to offset rising Social Security costs. Bad. This would make Social Security even more regressive since poor people don't live nearly as long as rich people.

7) LET THE MINIMUM WAGE CONTINUE TO DECLINE as inflation eats it away. Wrong again. Low-wage workers need a higher minimum wage.

Ryan is not just wrong, he's seven times wrong. §

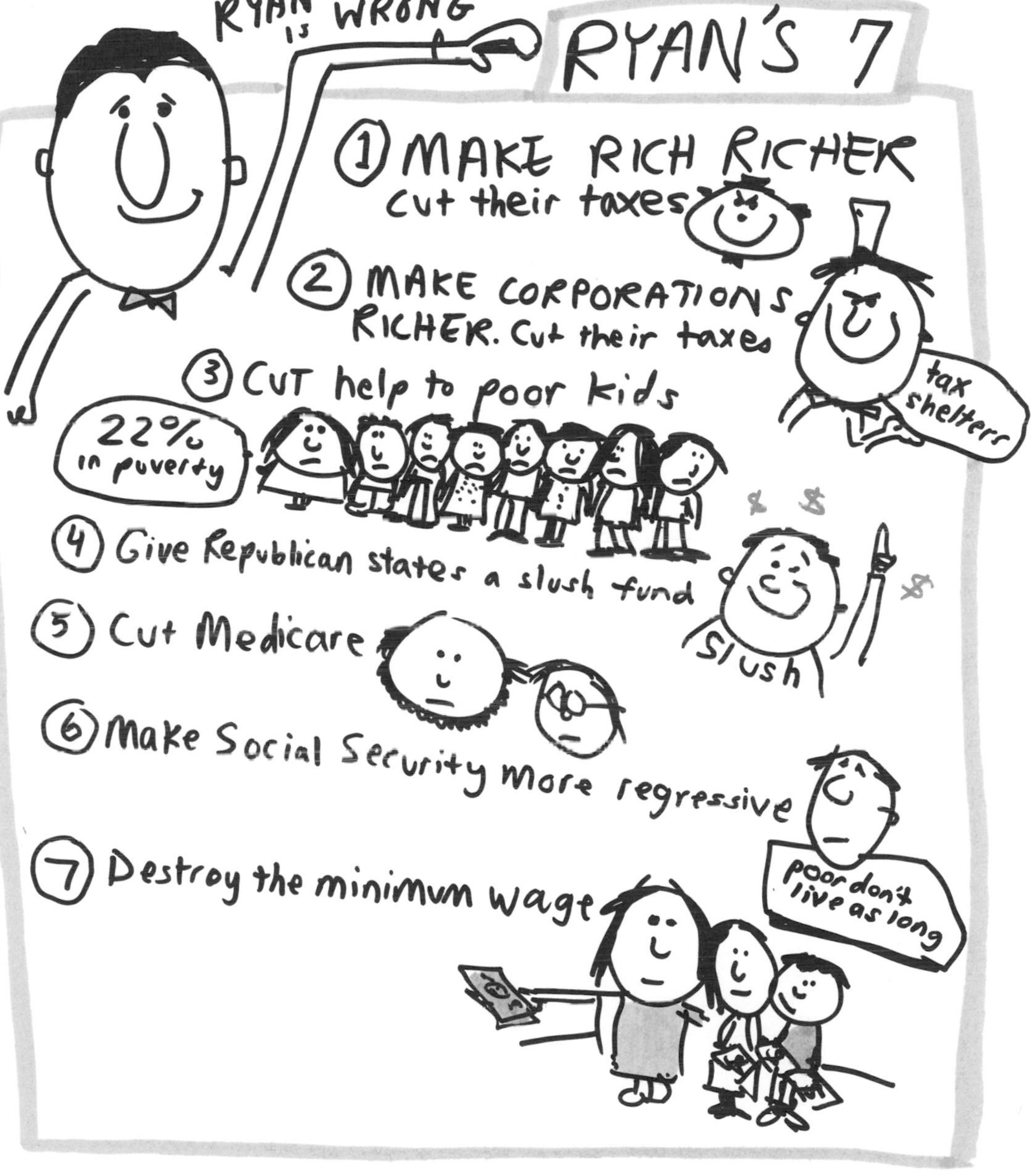
RYAN IS WRONG
RYAN'S 7
① MAKE RICH RICHER
Cut their taxes
② MAKE CORPORATIONS RICHER. Cut their taxes
tax shelters
③ CUT help to poor kids
22% in poverty
④ Give Republican states a slush fund
Slush
⑤ Cut Medicare
⑥ Make Social Security more regressive
poor don't live as long
⑦ Destroy the minimum wage

"RIGHT-TO-WORK" IS WRONG FOR WORKERS

So far this year, 16 state legislatures have introduced so-called "right-to-work" laws — which should really be called "right-to-work for less" laws — because they lead to lower wages and fewer benefits for most workers.

That's because the purpose of these laws is to destroy unions and undermine the bargaining power of average workers.

Here's how they work. Under the National Labor Relations Act of 1935, when a majority of workers votes for a union at the company that employs them, they're entitled to a have a union — and that union bargains with management for higher wages and better working conditions.

The union has bargaining clout because all workers at that company are represented by the union. That's what "union" means.

Obviously, in order to do the bargaining and make sure management adheres to the deal, a union has to have enough funds to keep it going. Which means all employees who benefit have to pay their share of the cost.

But the so-called "right-to-work" laws allow workers to get the benefits of belonging to a

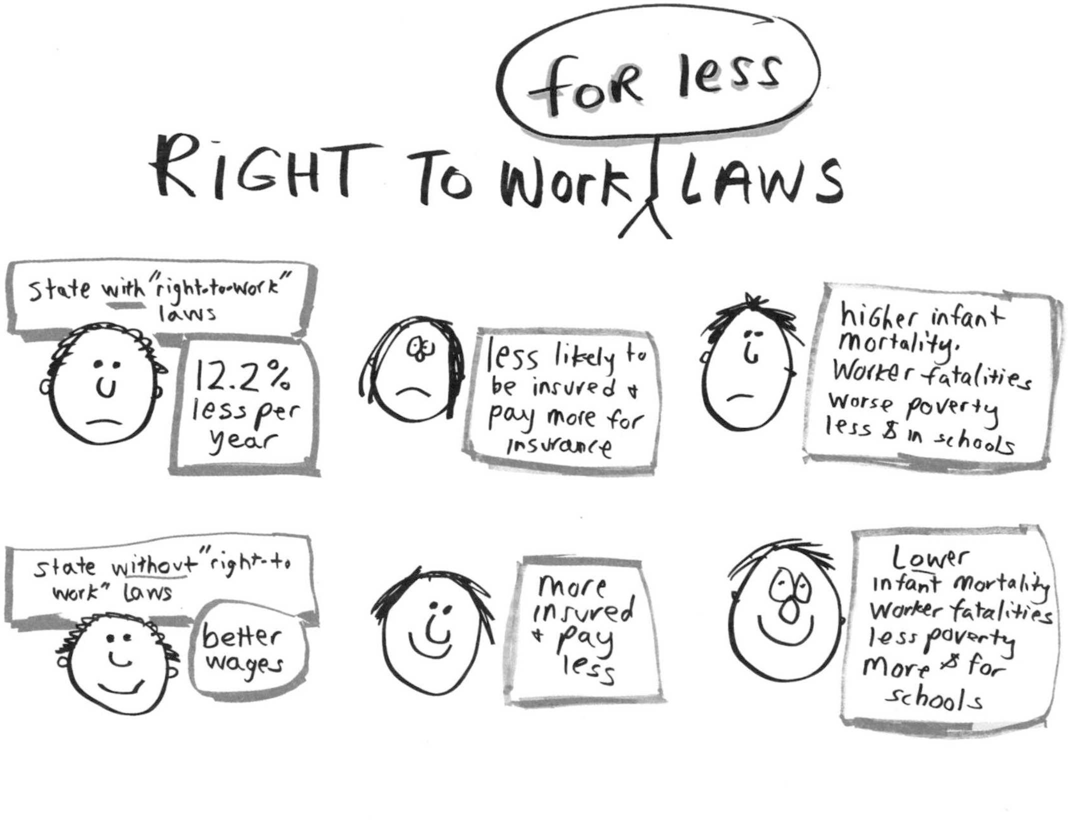
for less
RIGHT TO WORK LAWS
state with "right-to-work" laws
12.2% less per year
less likely to be insured + pay more for insurance
higher infant mortality, worker fatalities worse poverty less $ in schools
state without "right-to work" laws
better wages
more insured + pay less
Lower infant mortality worker fatalities less poverty more $ for schools

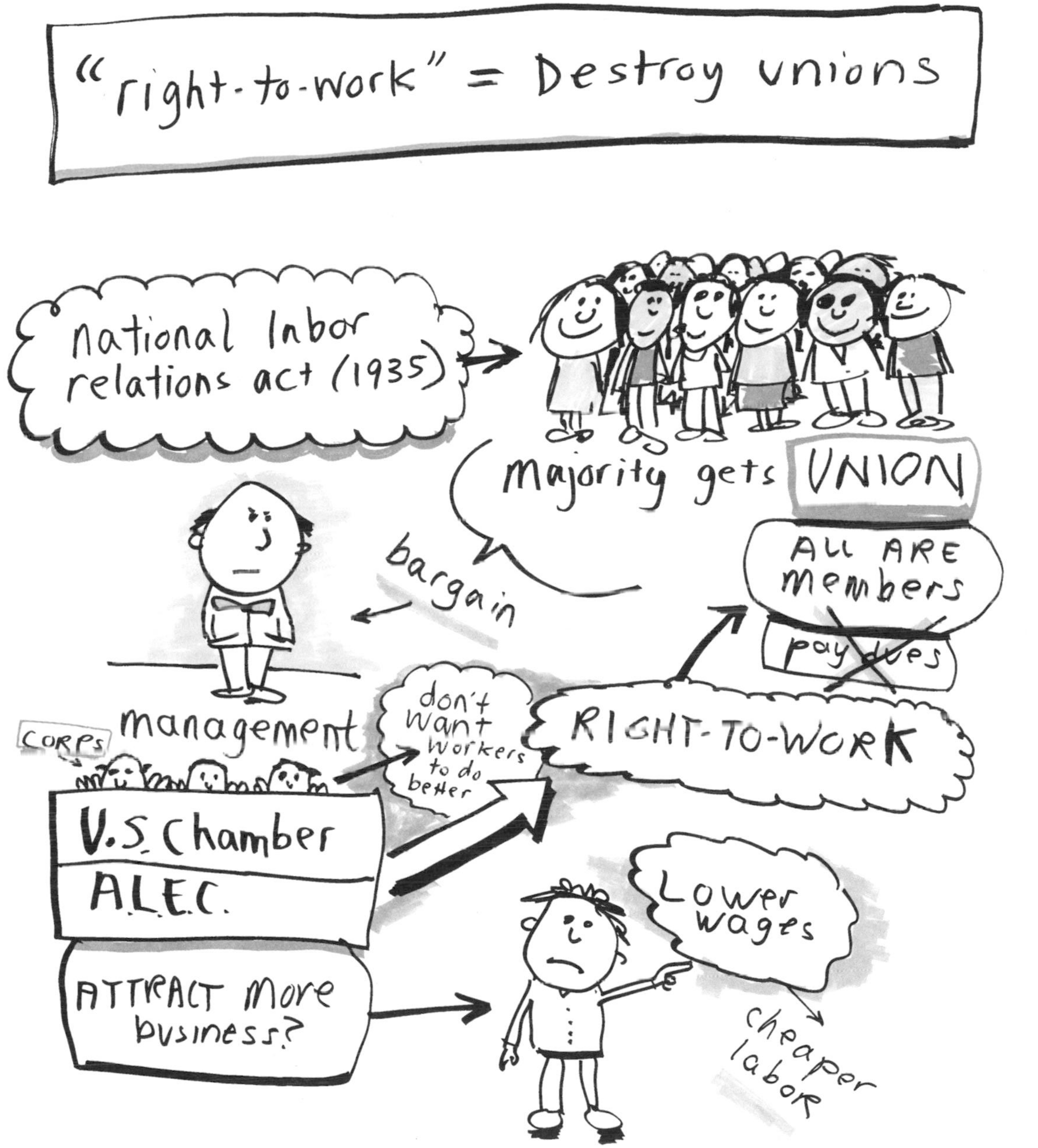
"right-to-work" = Destroy unions
national labor relations act (1935)
majority gets UNION
bargain
ALL ARE members
pay dues
management
CORPS
don't want workers to do better
RIGHT-TO-WORK
U.S. Chamber
A.L.E.C.
ATTRACT more business?
Lower wages
cheaper labor

union without paying — which means unions don't have the funds they need to keep the pressure on employers.

No wonder the U.S. Chamber of Commerce and the corporate-backed American Legislative Exchange Council (ALEC) are pushing these right-to-work laws. They argue that it's unfair to workers who don't want to be part of a union to have to pay union dues.

Who are they trying to fool? The Chamber of Commerce and ALEC represent corporations, not workers. The truth is, their corporate sponsors don't want American workers to have enough power to negotiate for higher wages, better schedules, and improved working conditions.

So it's no surprise that workers in so-called "right-to-work" states have lower pay and benefits than workers in states that don't have these corporate-sponsored laws.

The Chamber and ALEC say right-to-work states attract more businesses. The truth is they attract businesses that seek lower wages — businesses that don't invest in their workers, don't do research and development, don't add value, and therefore are the most likely to go abroad for even cheaper labor the first chance they can.

It's bad enough American wages have been stuck in the mud for three decades, while corporate profits have soared and top executive pay has gone through the stratosphere — and that almost all the economic gains have been going to the top 1%. So-called "right to work" laws are making all this even worse.

The only way average Americans are going to get a fair share of the gains is if they have more bargaining power — as they did 50 years ago when a third of all Americans in the private sector were unionized. Now, fewer than 7% are. We have to increase, not reduce, the bargaining power of average people.

So don't be fooled by the U.S. Chamber of Commerce and the American Legislative Exchange Council. They want your wages to drop so big shareholders and top executives can rake in even more. Don't let them. Join the fight against so-called "right-to-work" laws. §

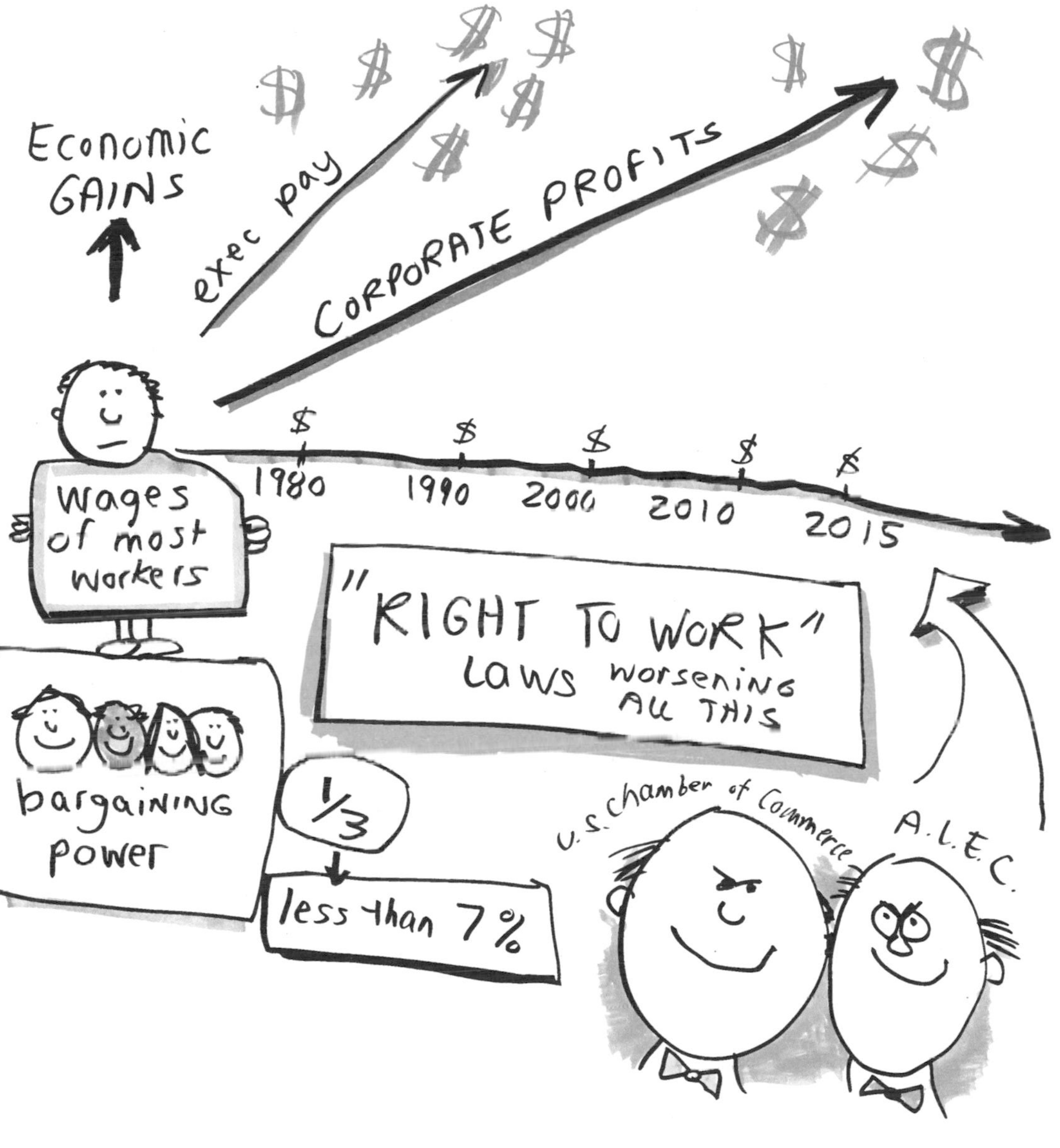
Economic GAINS
exec pay
CORPORATE PROFITS
wages of most workers
1980
1990
2000
2010
2015
"RIGHT TO WORK" laws worsening all this
bargaining power
1/3
less than 7%
U.S. Chamber of Commerce
A.L.E.C.

VOTER SUPPRESSION (AND HOW IT WORKS)

A crowning achievement of the historic March on Washington, where Dr. Martin Luther King Jr. gave his "I Have a Dream" speech, was pushing through the landmark Voting Rights Act of 1965. Recognizing the history of racist attempts to prevent black people from voting, that federal law forced a number of Southern states to adhere to federal guidelines allowing citizens access to the polls.

But in 2013, the Supreme Court effectively gutted many of these protections. As a result, states are finding new ways to stop more and more people, especially African Americans and other likely Democratic voters, from reaching the polls. Several states are requiring government-issued photo IDs, like driver's licenses, to vote, even though there's no evidence of the voter fraud this is supposed to prevent.

But there's plenty of evidence that these ID measures depress voting, especially among communities of color, young voters, and lower-income Americans. Alabama, after requiring photo IDs, has practically closed driver's license offices in counties with large percentages of black voters. Other states are reducing opportunities for early voting.

And several state legislatures, not just in the South, are gerrymandering districts to reduce the political power of people of color and Democrats, and thereby guarantee Republican control in Congress.

Here's one way they do it:
Here are 16 black dots and 12 white squares.

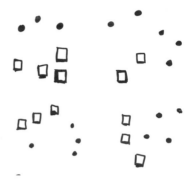

If districts were not gerrymandered, they might look like this: and three out of four would have black dot majorities.

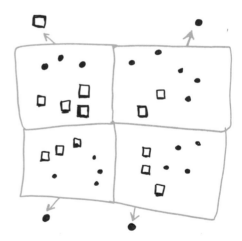

But after gerrymandering, using the exact same arrangement of dots and squares, three out of four have white square majorities.

We need to move to the next stage of voting rights: a new Voting Rights Act that renews the law that was effectively repealed by the conservative activists on the Supreme Court, sets minimum national standards, provides automatic voter registration when people get driver's licenses, allows at least two weeks of early voting — and takes districting away from the politicians and puts it under independent commissions.

Voting rights are too important to be left to partisan politics.

We must not allow anyone's vote to be taken away. §

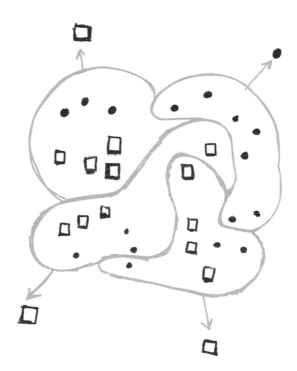

THE REPUBLICAN TAX SHAM

Watch your wallets. Republicans are pushing a new corporate tax plan that will end up costing most Americans a bundle. Here's what you should know about the so-called "border adjustment tax."

The U.S. imports about $2.7 trillion worth of goods each year. Many imports are cheap because labor costs are much lower in places like Southeast Asia.

Our current tax code taxes corporations on their profits. So, for example, when Wal-Mart buys T-shirts from Vietnam for $10 and sells them for $13, Wal-Mart is only taxed on that $3 of profit.

But under the new Republican tax plan, Wal-Mart would be taxed on the full price of imported items, so in this case the full $13 sale price of that T-shirt. As a result of this tax, Wall Street analysts expect retail prices in the U.S. to rise as much as 15%.

The plan would also cut taxes on companies that export from the United States. This is intended to encourage companies to locate production here in the United States.

But it wouldn't reverse the tide of automation that's rapidly eliminating jobs even from American factories.

The worst thing about the plan is that it is a hidden upward redistribution. Its burden will fall mainly on the poor and middle class because they already spend almost all of their incomes, so they will feel the greatest economic pain from higher retail prices.

The benefits will go to companies that export and their shareholders, who will benefit from the tax cuts in the form of higher profits — and higher share prices. Shareholders, who are mostly upper-income people, do not need this windfall.

Republicans claim that the U.S. dollar would rise in response to higher taxes on imports, effectively wiping out the tax burden.

But as a practical matter, no one knows if this will happen.

Bottom line: the tax plan is dressed up as a way to make America more competitive. But underneath it's just a typical Republican plan that redistributes from the poor and middle class to corporations and the wealthy. §

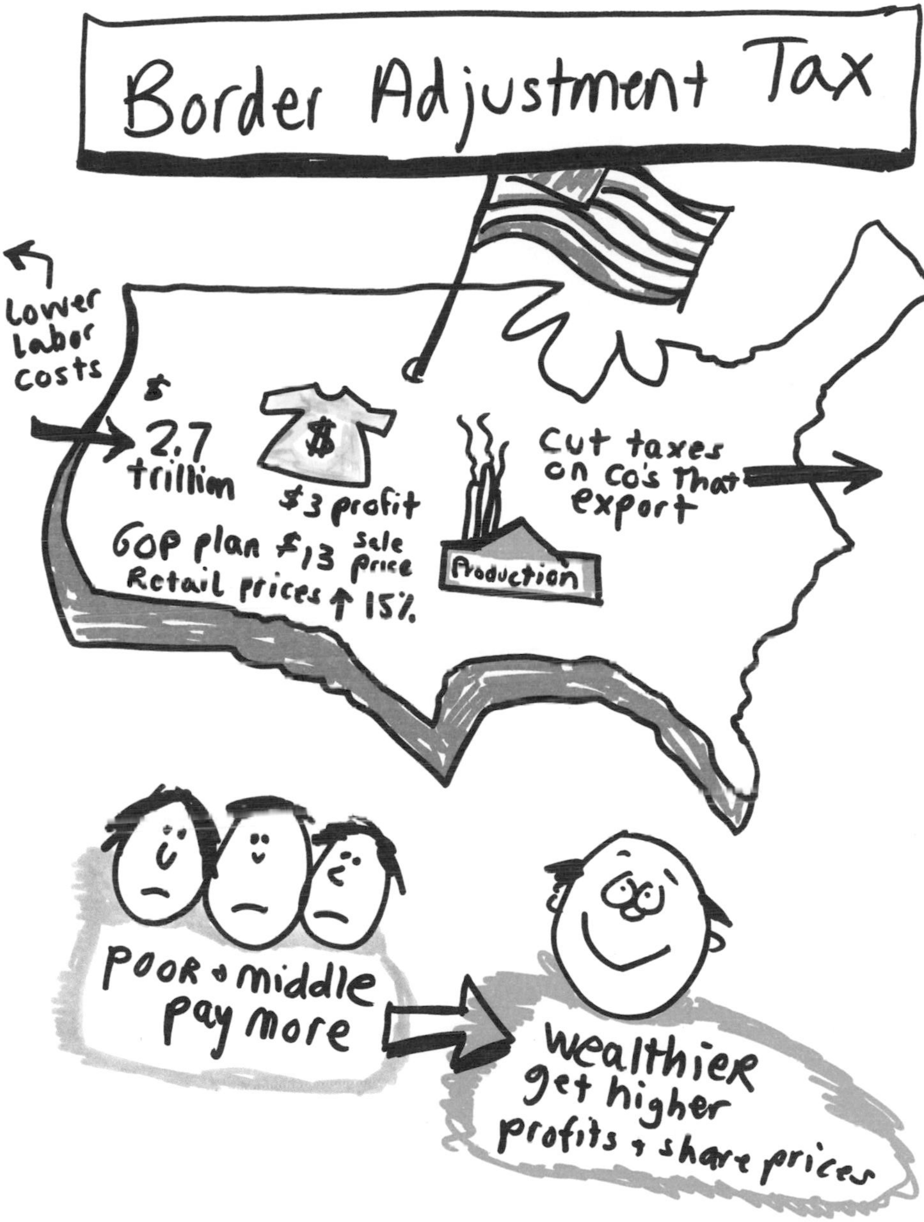
Border Adjustment Tax
Lower labor costs
$ 2.7 trillion
$
$3 profit
GOP plan $13 sale price
Retail prices ↑ 15%
Production
Cut taxes on Co's that export
POOR + middle pay more
wealthier get higher profits + share prices

AUSTERITY 101: THE THREE REASONS REPUBLICAN DEFICIT HAWKS ARE WRONG

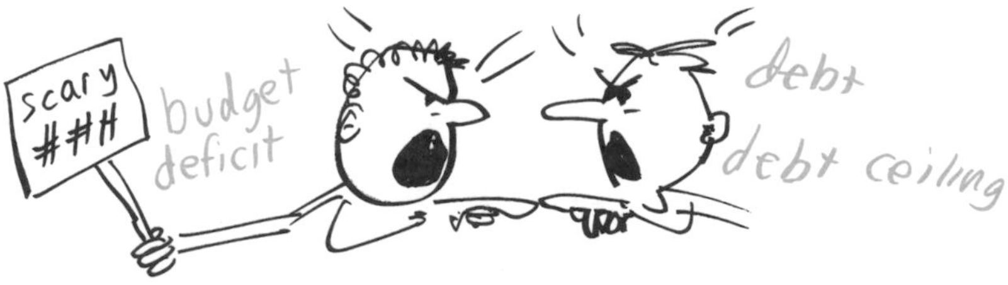
scary ###
budget deficit
debt
debt ceiling

Every time Congress gets into a big brawl over the federal budget deficit, the national debt, and the debt ceiling, deficit hawks run around waving scary numbers. The next time this happens, don't be fooled. Here are the three basic principles you need to know.

1) **DEFICIT AND DEBT NUMBERS ARE MEANINGLESS ON THEIR OWN.** They have to be viewed as a percent of the national economy. That ratio is critical. As long as the yearly deficit continues to drop as a percentage of the national economy — as it's been doing for several years now — we can more easily pay what we owe.

2) **AMERICA NEEDS TO RUN LARGER DEFICITS WHEN LOTS OF PEOPLE ARE UNEMPLOYED** or underemployed, as they still are today. Millions who remain too discouraged to look for jobs have dropped out of the workforce altogether, and millions more are in part-time jobs and need full time work. As we've known for years, in every economic downturn and in every struggling recovery, more government spending helps create jobs — teachers, firefighters, police officers, social workers, and other workers to rebuild roads and bridges and parks. Those jobs and that spending multiply through the economy.

Doing the opposite — cutting back spending when a lot of people are still out of work, as Congress has done with a sequester and as much of Europe has done — causes economies to slow or even shrink, which makes the deficit larger in proportion.

This is why austerity economics can be a recipe for disaster, as it has been in Greece. Creditors and institutions worried about Greece's debt forced it to cut spending. The spending cuts led

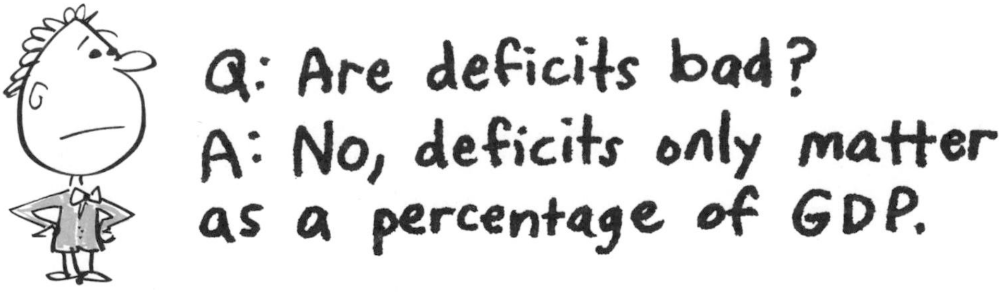
Q: Are deficits bad?
A: No, deficits only matter as a percentage of GDP.

to a huge economic recession, which reduced tax revenues and made the debt crisis there even worse than it had been before the cuts.

3) **DEFICIT SPENDING ON INVESTMENTS LIKE EDUCATION AND INFRASTRUCTURE IS DIFFERENT** than other forms of spending because this spending — investment spending — builds productivity and future economic growth. It's like a family borrowing money to send a kid to college or start a business. If the likely return on the investment exceeds the borrowing costs, it should be done.

Keep these three principles in mind, and you won't be fooled by the scare tactics of the deficit hawks. And you'll understand why we have to end the sequester, put more people to work, and increase rather than decrease spending on vital public investments such as education and infrastructure. §

1
deficit · debt
GDP
ratio
up
down
2
More spending needed
Creates jobs
too discouraged to look... or need full-time jobs
unemployed or under-employed: need work
GROWS
economy:
deficit or debt
GDP
ratio drops
OR
Slow or shrink
ratio worsens
cut spending
recession
reduced tax revenues
worsening the crisis
GREECE
3
INVESTMENT spending
Start-up
if returns exceed borrowing costs
Yes!

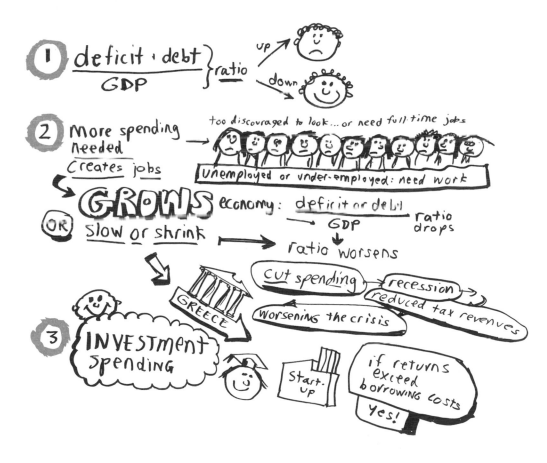

THE REAL REASON REPUBLICANS WANT TO PULL THE PLUG ON OBAMACARE

Don't be hoodwinked by the promises of Trump and the Republicans to "repeal and replace" Obamacare. They could repeal it, but they can't and won't replace it. They've tried for years to come up with a replacement that keeps at least as many people covered. Their "replacement" never appears.

So why do Republicans want to repeal Obamacare and leave millions without insurance? Because it would mean a huge tax windfall for the wealthy.

Repealing Obamacare would put an average $33,000 tax cut into the hands of the richest one percent (1%) in the first year alone, and a whopping $197,000 average tax cut into the hands of the top one-tenth of one percent (0.01%).

The 400 highest-income taxpayers (with incomes averaging more than $300 million each) will each receive an average annual tax cut of about $7 million.

It would also increase the taxes of families earning between $10,000 and $75,000 — including just about all of Trump's working-class voters.

So what do we end up with when Republicans repeal Obamacare?

- 32 million people losing their health insurance
- Tens of thousands of Americans dying because they don't get the medical care they need
- Medicare in worse shape
- And the rich becoming far richer.

This is lunacy. We must stand up to it. §

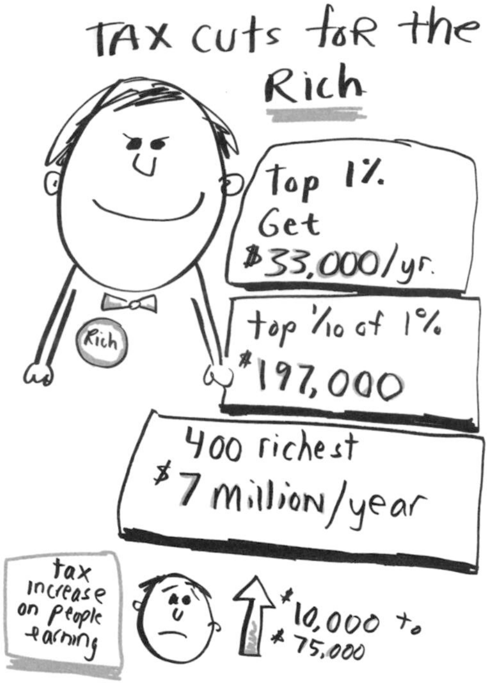
TAX cuts for the Rich
top 1% Get $33,000/yr.
top 1/10 of 1% $197,000
400 richest $7 Million/year
Rich
tax increase on people earning
$10,000 to $75,000

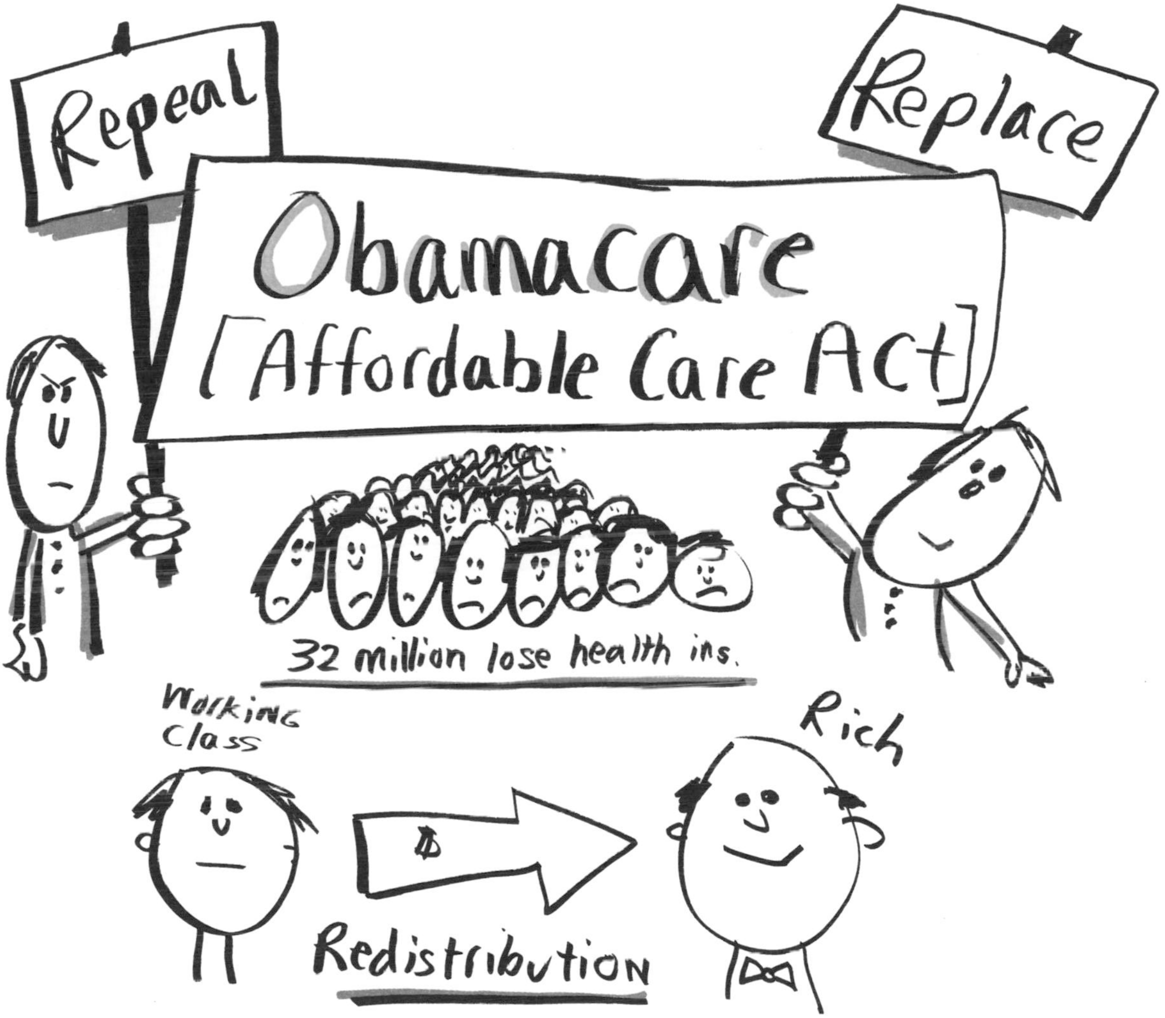
Repeal
Replace
Obamacare
[Affordable Care Act]
32 million lose health ins.
Working Class
Rich
$
Redistribution

HANDS OFF MY MEDICARE!

Speaker of the House Paul Ryan plans to begin the Medicare phase-out he has long advocated — packaged together with the repeal of the Affordable Care Act.

Ryan aims to replace Medicare with vouchers that seniors would use to buy private insurance. This Republican attack on Medicare will offer Democrats a golden opportunity to turn the tide and take back Congress. But Democrats have to be smart enough to seize the opportunity and act on it.

NOW, AS PART OF HIS STRATEGY, RYAN WILL TRY TO CONVINCE THE PUBLIC OF THESE LIES:

1. RYAN SAYS MEDICARE IS ALL BUT DEAD ALREADY, which is why he says things like, "Because of Obamacare [the Affordable Care Act], Medicare is going broke."

Rubbish. In fact, the ACA has extended the solvency of the Medicare trust fund by more than a decade.

2. RYAN SAYS SENIORS SHOULDN'T WORRY because the changes won't take effect for years.

Baloney. Medicare is hugely popular with younger people who see how important it is for their parents and grandparents. Remember the Tea Partiers who protested against the Affordable Care Act with signs that said "Don't Touch My Medicare"?

3. RYAN SAYS VOUCHERS WILL BE JUST AS GOOD AS MEDICARE.

A lie. If seniors can't afford to buy any of the available plans with what the voucher is worth, they're out of luck. And the vouchers won't keep up with increases in the costs of healthcare.

4. RYAN SAYS SENIORS WHO WANT TO CAN REMAIN ON MEDICARE.

More rubbish. The Ryan plan is designed to lure healthier seniors out of Medicare, leaving the most unhealthy and costliest behind — thereby drowning Medicare in a sea of red ink.

This is a pivotal issue. Progressives have a winning message, but we have to make sure the public knows the facts. Tell Paul Ryan and the Republicans: Keep your hands off our Medicare. §

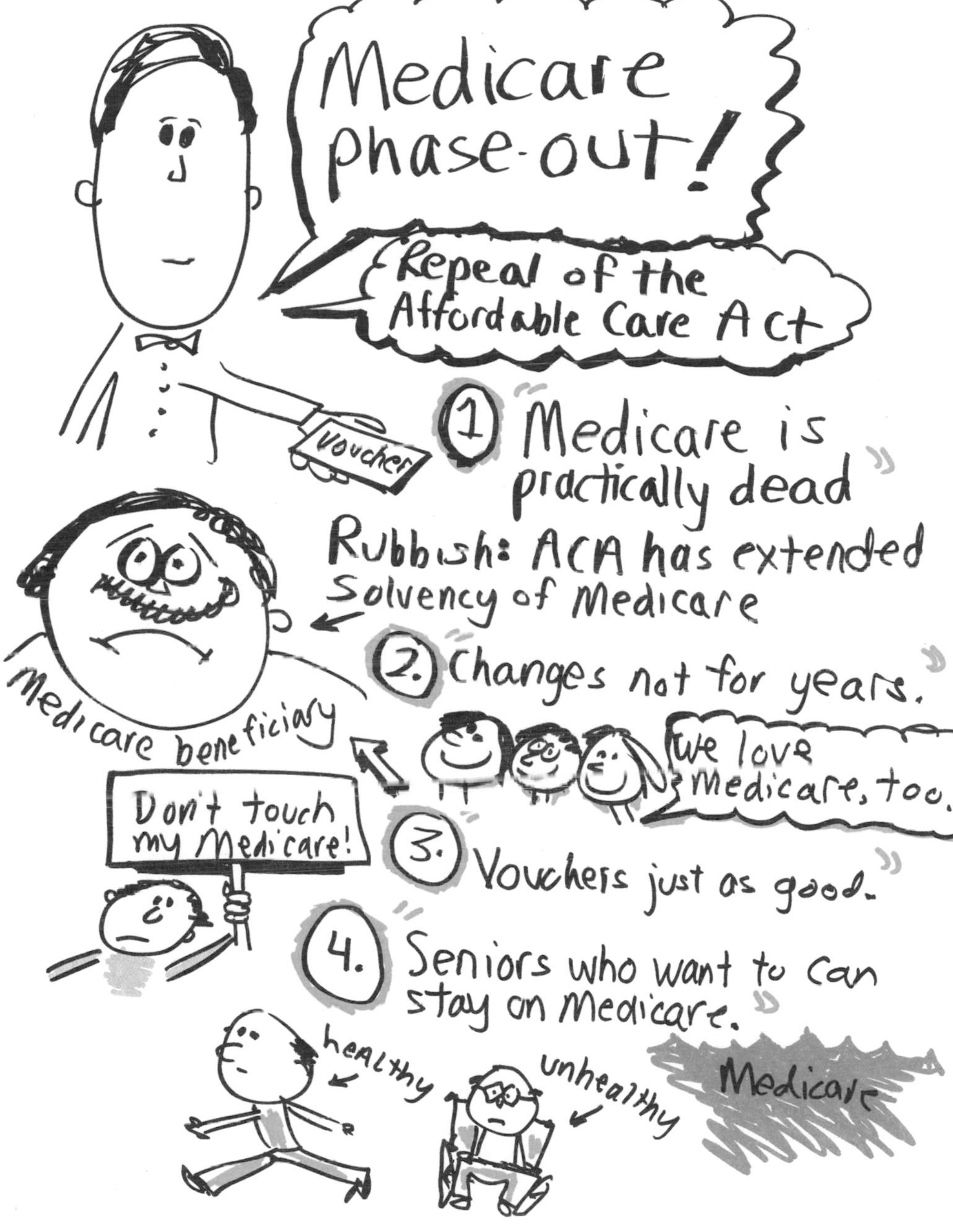

Medicare phase-out!
Repeal of the Affordable Care Act
Voucher
1 Medicare is practically dead
Rubbish: ACA has extended Solvency of Medicare
Medicare beneficiary
2. Changes not for years.
We love Medicare, too!
Don't touch my Medicare!
3. Vouchers just as good.
4. Seniors who want to can stay on Medicare.
healthy
unhealthy
Medicare

THE COST OF WAR

Some politicians say diplomacy with Iran isn't worth it; that we should use our military might instead. Yet every day, nuclear non-proliferation experts, national security experts, U.S. ambassadors, top American scientists, and high-ranking military officials add their voices to a growing chorus of support for diplomacy with Iran, declaring that the Iran deal is solid and will make our nation more secure.

The fact is, if we don't use diplomacy, the alternative is war. War should only be our last resort. Diplomacy — vigorous, muscular diplomacy — should always be what we try first. I'm not a pacifist. I look at hard facts: risks, numbers, benefits, costs. The most obvious cost of war is lives lost (on all sides) and painful, lasting trauma — civilians killed and maimed, children orphaned, refugees, festering resentments.

But there are other costs to war as well — measured in what we cannot do for our own people here in America because of what we spend on war and the resulting expansion of our nation's military reach.

In 2017, military spending will account for more than half of all federal discretionary spending — spending that the president requests and lawmakers appropriate. The United States spends more on the military than the next seven largest military budgets around the world combined.

But we can't be a strong nation if we're not strong at home, and we can't be strong at home when almost one in five of our children live in poverty, our schools are in disrepair, our roads and bridges are falling apart, our water and sewage systems are outmoded, and healthcare is still unavailable to millions.

Nobel Laureate Joseph Stiglitz estimates that the war in Iraq cost us 3 trillion dollars, including direct government expenses; the cost of diagnosing, treating, and compensating disabled veterans; and the war's broader impact on the U.S. economy and the national debt. If we go to war with Iran and that war costs only what the war in Iraq cost — just the bare minimum, mind you, not the extended costs — we won't be able to invest in America. We can't rebuild America.

Finally, there is never a guarantee that war will succeed. We've been at war in the Middle East for more than 12 years. America will soon have a generation raised entirely during wartime with no prospect of an end in sight.

If diplomacy with Iran is an option, we must use it for the sake of our children, for peace in the world. §

Federal discretionary spending
other
Military
China
Russia
Germany
G.B.
Fr
Middle East
Saudi Arabia
Sp
$

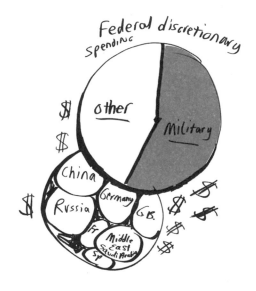

The US spends more on the military than the next seven largest military budgets around the world combined.

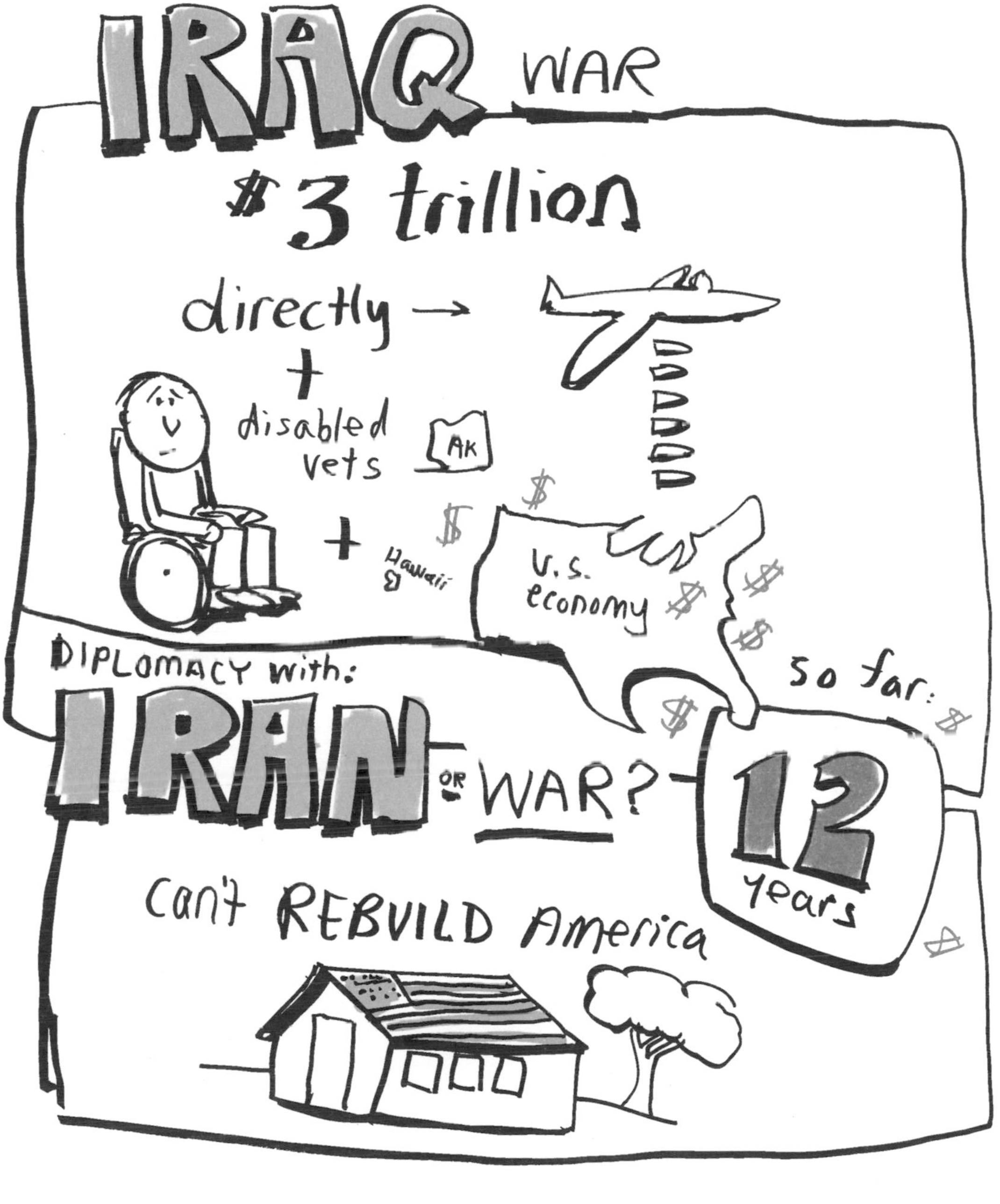
IRAQ WAR
$3 trillion
directly →
+
disabled vets
AK
+
Hawaii
U.S. economy
DIPLOMACY with:
IRAN OR WAR?
so far: $
12 years
can't REBUILD America

CLIMATE AND INEQUALITY

Climate change and widening inequality are not separate issues. They're intimately connected. And there's at least one solution to both.

The people who are bearing the brunt of climate change here and around the world are the poor and working class who live in areas increasingly prone to flooding. Who rely on croplands susceptible to ever-more frequent droughts. Who depend on outdated water and sewage systems, and older roadways and power grids that are falling apart under the strains of more severe weather. Who live in fragile structures particularly vulnerable to intensifying hurricanes and violent storms. Whose health is especially compromised by airborne contaminants, infections, and other diseases that accompany climate change.

So what do we do?

You often hear that reversing climate change will mean fewer jobs, especially for the poor and working class — the very people who are bearing the biggest burden from climate change.

But that's not true. Clean energy — powered by wind, or solar cells, or water — is growing fast, even as the old fossil-fuel industries decline and generate fewer jobs. More than three times as many people are already employed generating electricity from solar and wind than from coal, oil, and gas combined. "Wind turbine technician" is our country's fastest-growing occupation.

This transition to renewables is inevitable, in part because of the so-called "beautiful math" of solar power: every time the world's solar power doubles, the cost of panels falls 26%. This has led to a 99% decline in the cost of solar modules since 1976 and an 80% decline since 2008 alone.

Donald Trump and his Republican enablers are afraid of clean energy because it puts power — literally and figuratively — back into the hands of people and communities. Their attacks on science and on health protections are just efforts to maintain billions of dollars in unjust profits and corporate giveaways for the barons of oil, gas, and coal and to undermine the urgency and speed of a transition already underway.

Reversing both climate change and inequality can be a win-win proposition. §

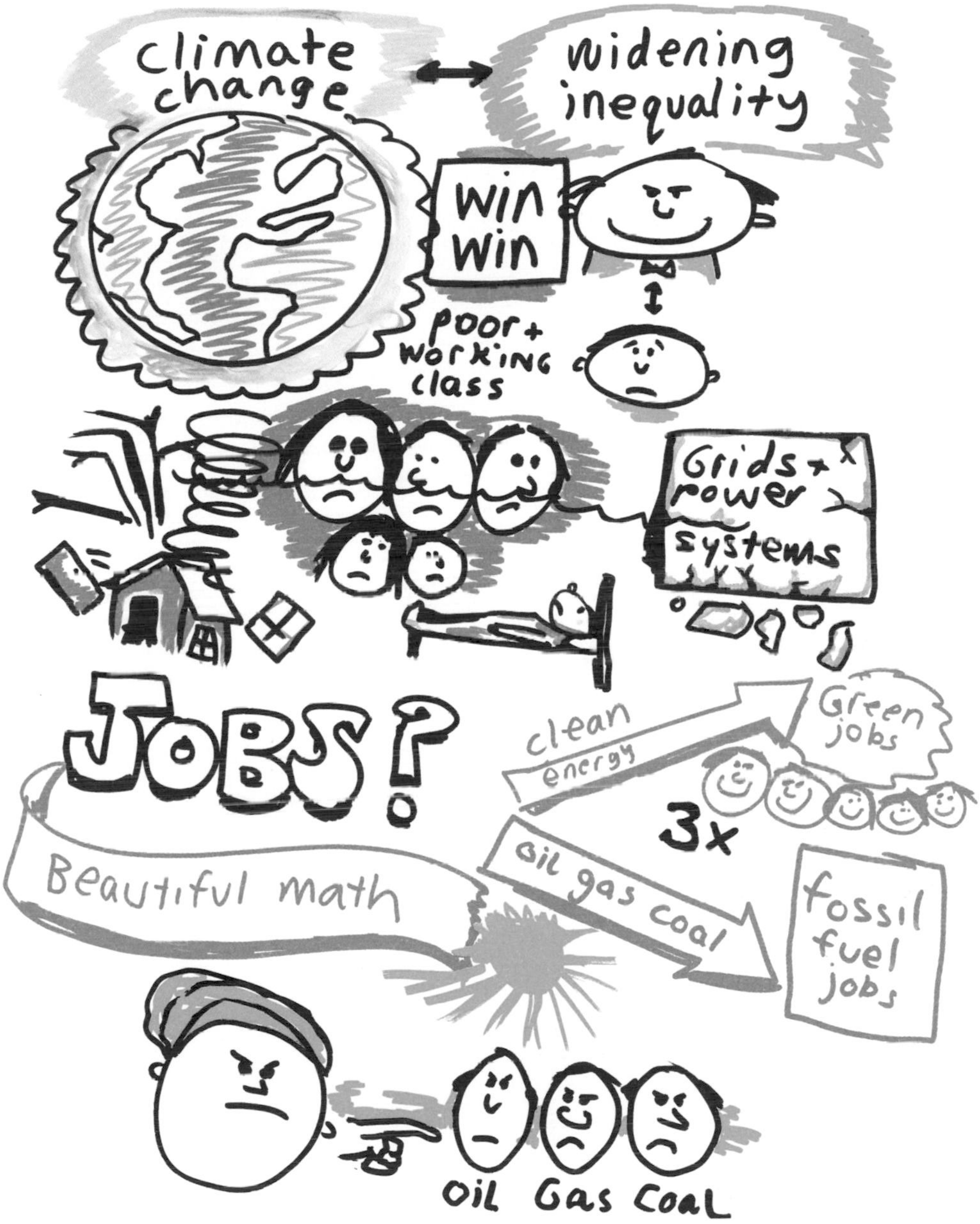
climate change
widening inequality
win win
poor + working class
Grids + power systems
JOBS?
Beautiful math
clean energy
Green jobs
3x
oil gas coal
fossil fuel jobs
Oil Gas Coal

THE FACTS ABOUT IMMIGRATION

Donald Trump has opened the floodgates to lies about immigration. Here are the myths — and the facts:

MYTH: IMMIGRANTS TAKE AWAY AMERICAN JOBS.

Wrong. Immigrants add to overall economic demand, and by doing so they thereby push companies to create more jobs.

MYTH: WE DON'T NEED ANY MORE IMMIGRANTS.

Baloney. The U.S. population is aging. Twenty-five years ago, each retiree in America was matched by five workers. Now for each retiree, there are only three workers. Without more immigration, in 15 years the ratio will fall to two workers for every retiree, which is not nearly enough to sustain our retiree population.

MYTH: IMMIGRANTS ARE A DRAIN ON PUBLIC BUDGETS.

Bull. Immigrants pay taxes! The Institute on Taxation and Economic Policy released a report in 2015 showing undocumented immigrants paid $11.8 billion in state and local taxes in 2012, and their combined nationwide state and local tax contributions would increase by $2.2 billion under comprehensive immigration reform.

MYTH: LEGAL AND ILLEGAL IMMIGRATION IS INCREASING.

Wrong again. The net rate of illegal immigration into the United States is less than zero. The number of undocumented immigrants living in the U.S. has declined from 12.2 million in 2007 to 11.3 million now, according to data from the Pew Research Center.

Don't listen to the demagogues who want to blame the economic problems of the middle class and poor on new immigrants, whether here legally or illegally. The real problem is that the economic game is rigged in favor of a handful at the top — who are doing the rigging.

We need to pass comprehensive immigration reform, giving those who are undocumented a path to citizenship. Scapegoating them, and other immigrants, is shameful.

And it's just plain wrong. §

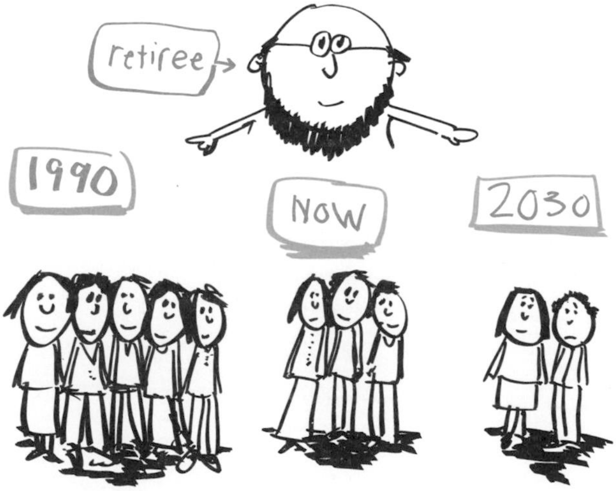
retiree
1990
NOW
2030

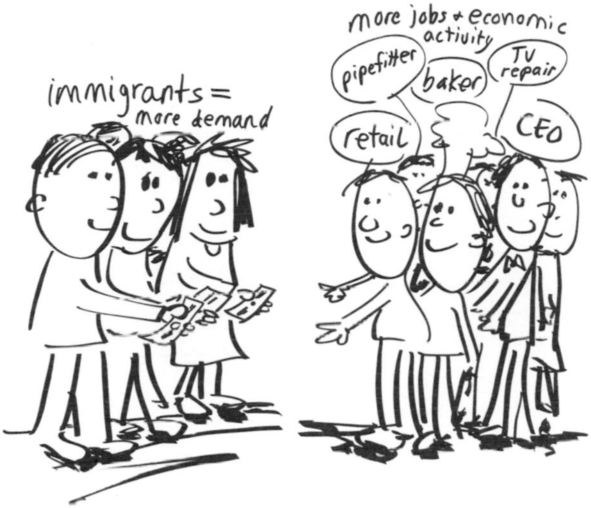
immigrants =
more demand
more jobs + economic activity
pipefitter
baker
TV repair
retail
CEO

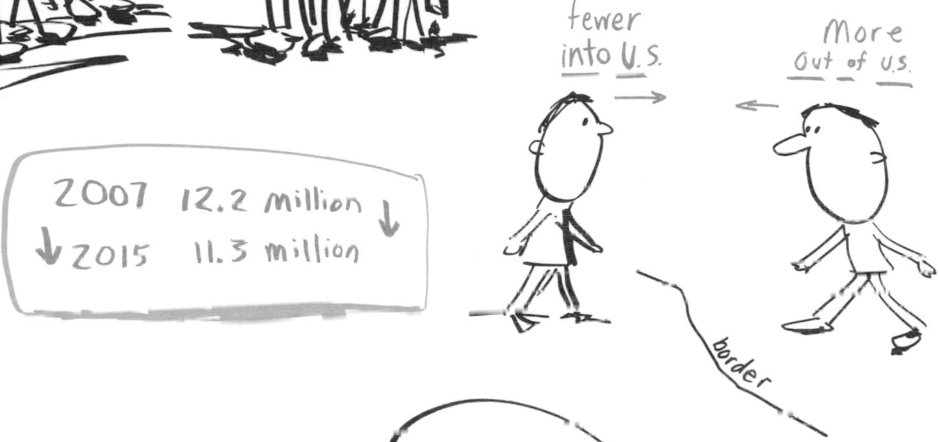
fewer into U.S.
More out of U.S.
2007 12.2 million
2015 11.3 million
border

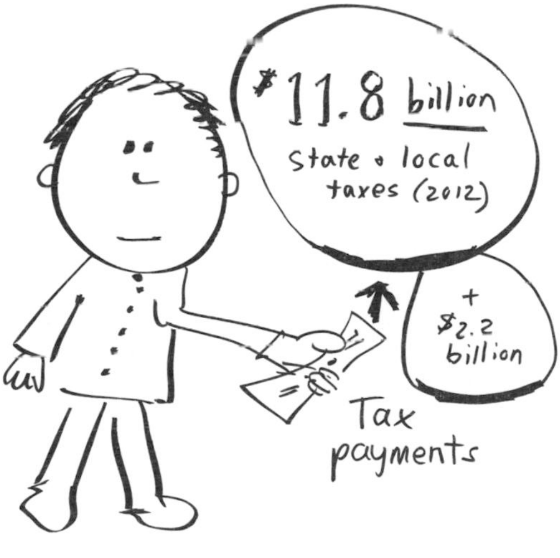
$11.8 billion
state + local taxes (2012)
+ $2.2 billion
Tax payments

WORD OF THE YEAR: XENOPHOBIA

Each year the folks at Dictionary.com look for a word that trended during the year and which is especially important — and pick it as their Word of the Year.

Their pick for 2016 is the word "Xenophobia." It means an unreasonable fear or hatred of foreigners, people from different cultures, or strangers.

Xenophobia can be seen as a reaction to a rise in globalization. Xenophobia is increasing around the world — just look at the Syrian refugee crisis, South African unrest, and Brexit. Xenophobia is also seeping into our own country, despite the fact that America has always been a nation of people from different places, different cultures, different races, different creeds. We've been the world's "melting pot."

A phrase engraved on our national monuments and even on our money is "E Pluribus Unum" — "out of many come one." I don't want to pretend American assimilation of foreigners has always been easy or faultless. White European settlers fought and killed Native Americans, stealing their land. Some Americans collaborated in kidnapping black people from Africa and forcing them into slavery here.

In the 19th century, Chinese workers in the West were discriminated against and excluded. Waves of immigrants from Italy and Ireland and Poland were initially met with hostility.

Although Emma Lazarus's famous words on the Statue of Liberty — "Give me your tired, your poor, your huddled masses yearning to breathe free" — told the world we welcomed immigrants, we didn't always act as if we did.

But we have at least striven toward tolerance and equal opportunity. We enacted voting rights and civil rights, and barred discrimination based on race, ethnicity, or nationality.

But in recent years, as wages stagnated and economic forces began to make many Americans afraid, some politicians used that fear. They channeled it into xenophobia — fear of the other. Fear of African Americans, fear of Mexicans, fear of Muslims.

Such scapegoating is not new in the history of the world. But it is dangerous. It divides us. It invites harassment and bullying, or worse. It turns us from tolerance and empathy to disrespect and hate.

Dictionary.com is right to make "Xenophobia" the word of the year, but it is also one of the biggest threats we face.

It is not a word to be celebrated. It is a sentiment to be fought. §

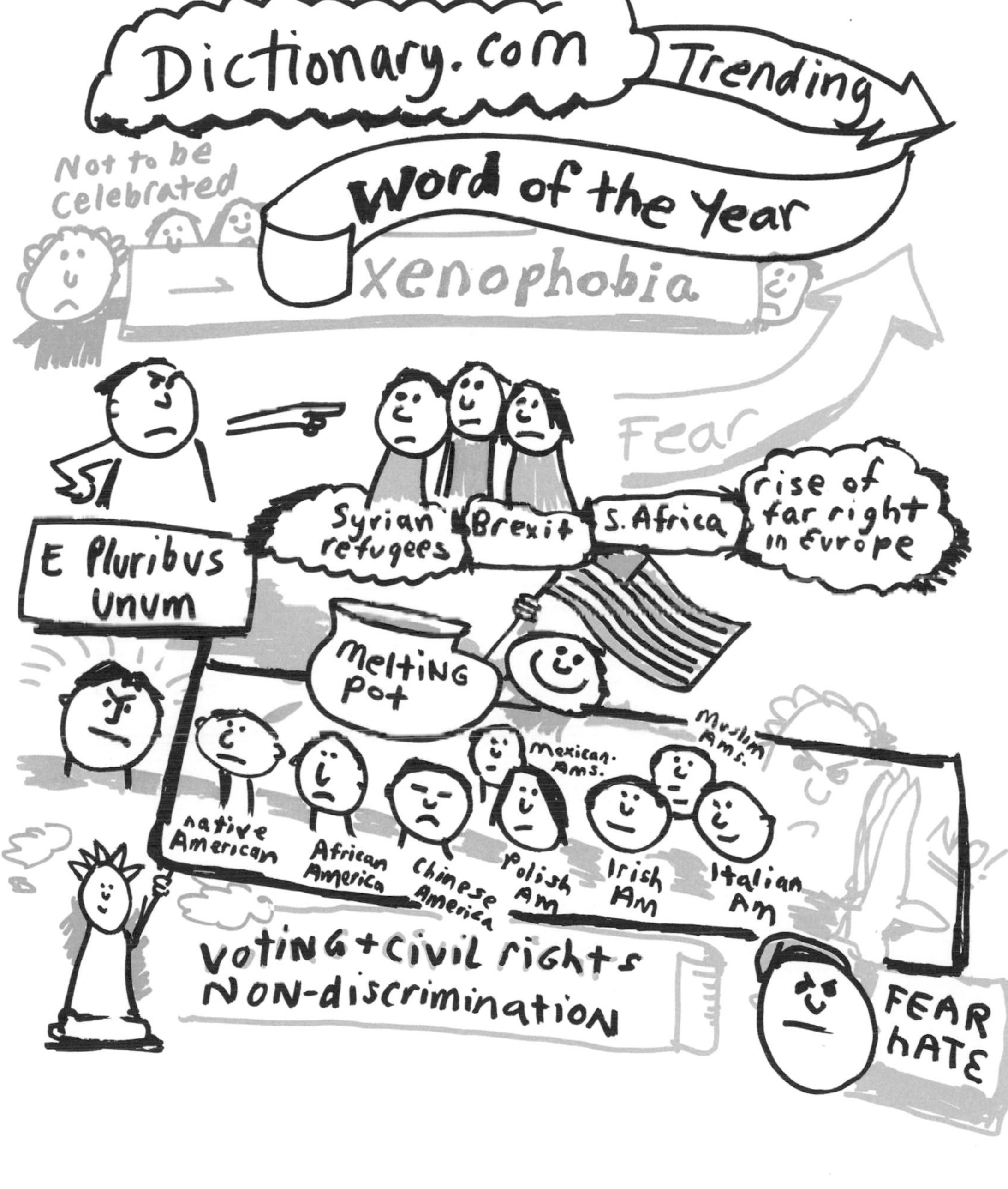

Dictionary.com
Trending
Word of the Year
Not to be Celebrated
xenophobia
Fear
Syrian refugees
Brexit
S. Africa
rise of far right in Europe
E Pluribus Unum
melting pot
Muslim Ams.
Mexican-Ams.
native American
African America
Chinese America
Polish Am
Irish Am
Italian Am
voting + civil rights
NON-discrimination
FEAR
hATE

SOLUTIONS

THE FIVE PRINCIPLES OF PATRIOTISM

We talk a lot about patriotism, especially around July 4th, but we also need to take to heart its five basic principles.

FIRST, TRUE PATRIOTISM ISN'T SIMPLY ABOUT WAVING THE AMERICAN FLAG. And it's not mostly about securing our borders, putting up walls, keeping others out. True patriotism is about coming together for the common good.

SECOND, PATRIOTISM ISN'T CHEAP. It requires taking on a fair share of the burdens of keeping America going, being willing to pay taxes in full rather than seeking tax loopholes and squirreling away money abroad. Patriotism means not just voting, but becoming politically active — volunteering time and energy to improving this country.

THIRD, PATRIOTISM IS ABOUT PRESERVING, FORTIFYING, AND PROTECTING OUR DEMOCRACY, not inundating it with big money and buying off politicians. It means defending the right to vote and ensuring more Americans are heard, not fewer.

FOURTH, TRUE PATRIOTS DON'T HATE THE GOVERNMENT OF THE UNITED STATES. They're proud of their country. They know the government is a tool to help us solve our problems together. They may not like everything it does, and they justifiably worry when special interests gain too much power. But true patriots work to improve our government, not destroy it.

FINALLY, PATRIOTS DON'T PANDER TO DIVISIVENESS. They don't fuel racist or religious or ethnic divisions. They aren't homophobic or sexist or racist. To the contrary, true patriots seek to confirm and strengthen and celebrate the "We" in "We the people of the United States." §

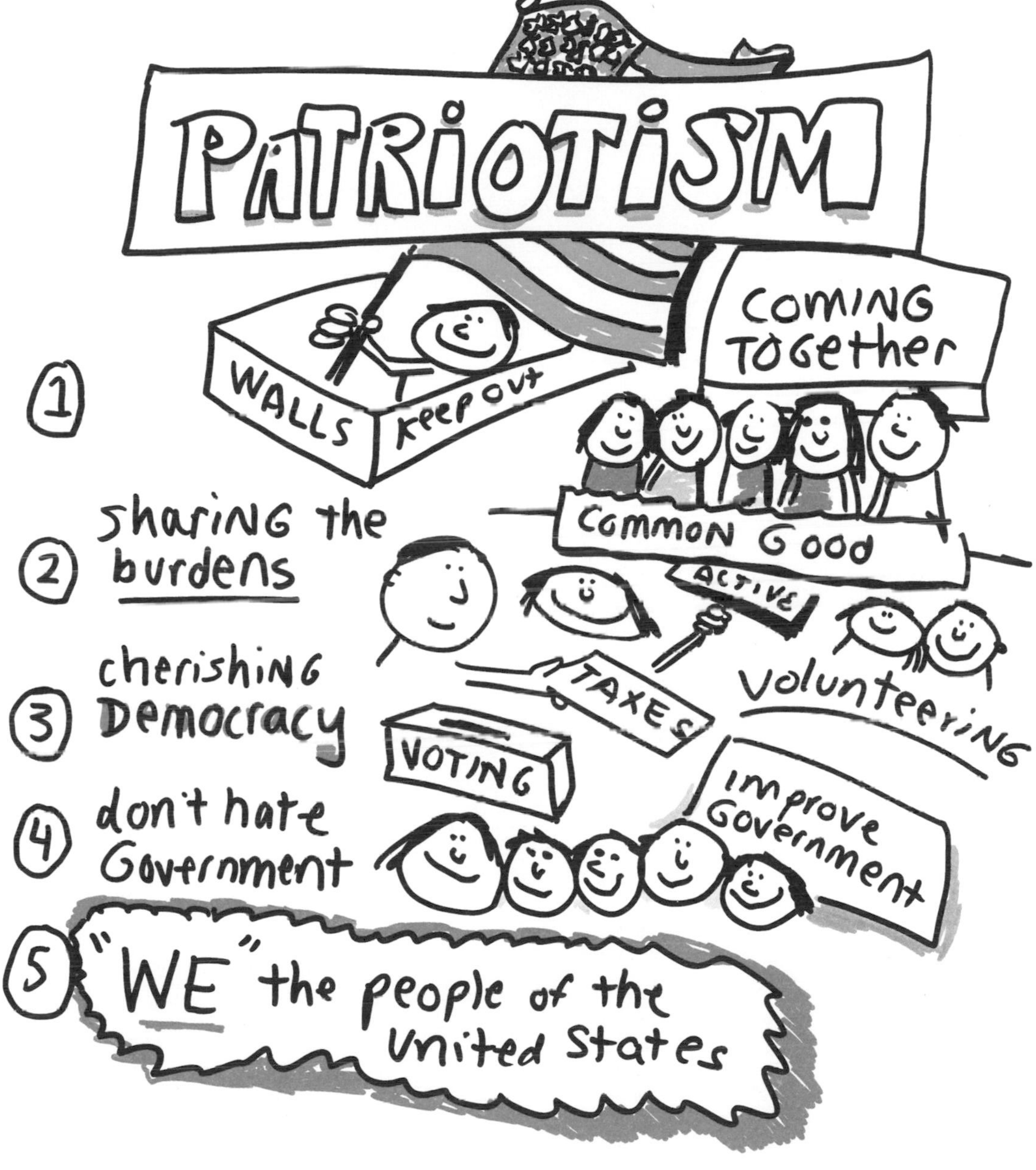
PATRIOTISM
COMING TOGether
WALLS
KEEP OUT
1
COMMON GOOD
sharing the burdens
2
ACTIVE
TAXES
volunteering
cherishing Democracy
3
VOTING
improve Government
don't hate Government
4
5
"WE" the people of the United States

RAISE THE MINIMUM WAGE TO $15 AN HOUR

The minimum wage should be raised to $15.00 an hour, incrementally, over the next three years. Here are seven reasons why:

1) HAD THE MINIMUM WAGE OF 1968 BEEN ADJUSTED FOR INFLATION, it would be well above $10.10 an hour today — but the typical worker today is more than twice as productive as the typical worker of 1968. Adjusted for both inflation and productivity gains, therefore, the minimum wage should be at least $15 an hour.

2) $10.10 AN HOUR IS NOT ENOUGH TO LIFT ALL WORKERS AND THEIR FAMILIES OUT OF POVERTY. This is especially true for millions of low-wage workers who want full-time jobs but can only work and find part-time work. Most low-wage workers are not teenagers. They're major breadwinners for their families.

3) SOME EMPLOYERS PAY WAGES THAT WILL NOT LIFT THEIR EMPLOYEES OUT OF POVERTY. The rest of us pay for those employees' Medicaid, food stamps, housing, and other assistance. In effect, we subsidize those low-wage businesses with our tax dollars. Some, like McDonald's, actually advise their employees to use public programs because their pay is just too low.

4) SOME JOBS MAY BE LOST IF THE MINIMUM IS RAISED TO $15, BUT many more people will be lifted out of poverty. And because low-wage workers will have more money to spend, their spending will create many more jobs.

5) A WAGE INCREASE IS MORE LIKELY TO COME OUT OF PROFITS THAN BE PASSED ON TO YOU in higher prices because most employers of low-wage workers are in intense competition for customers.

6) REPUBLICANS WOULD NO DOUBT ARGUE FOR NO INCREASE — or a minimal one from the current $7.25 to, say, $8.00 — so it's doubly important to be clear about what's right. Democrats should push for a big increase, not give credibility to Republican demands for a small one.

7) AT A TIME IN OUR NATION'S HISTORY when 95% of all economic gains are going to the top 1%, raising the minimum wage to $15.00 an hour isn't just smart economics, it's the right thing to do. §

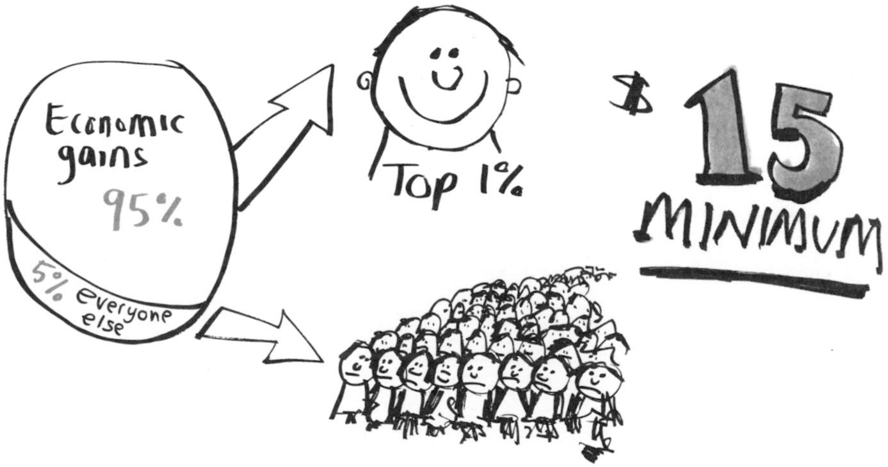
Economic gains
95%
5% everyone else
Top 1%
$15
MINIMUM

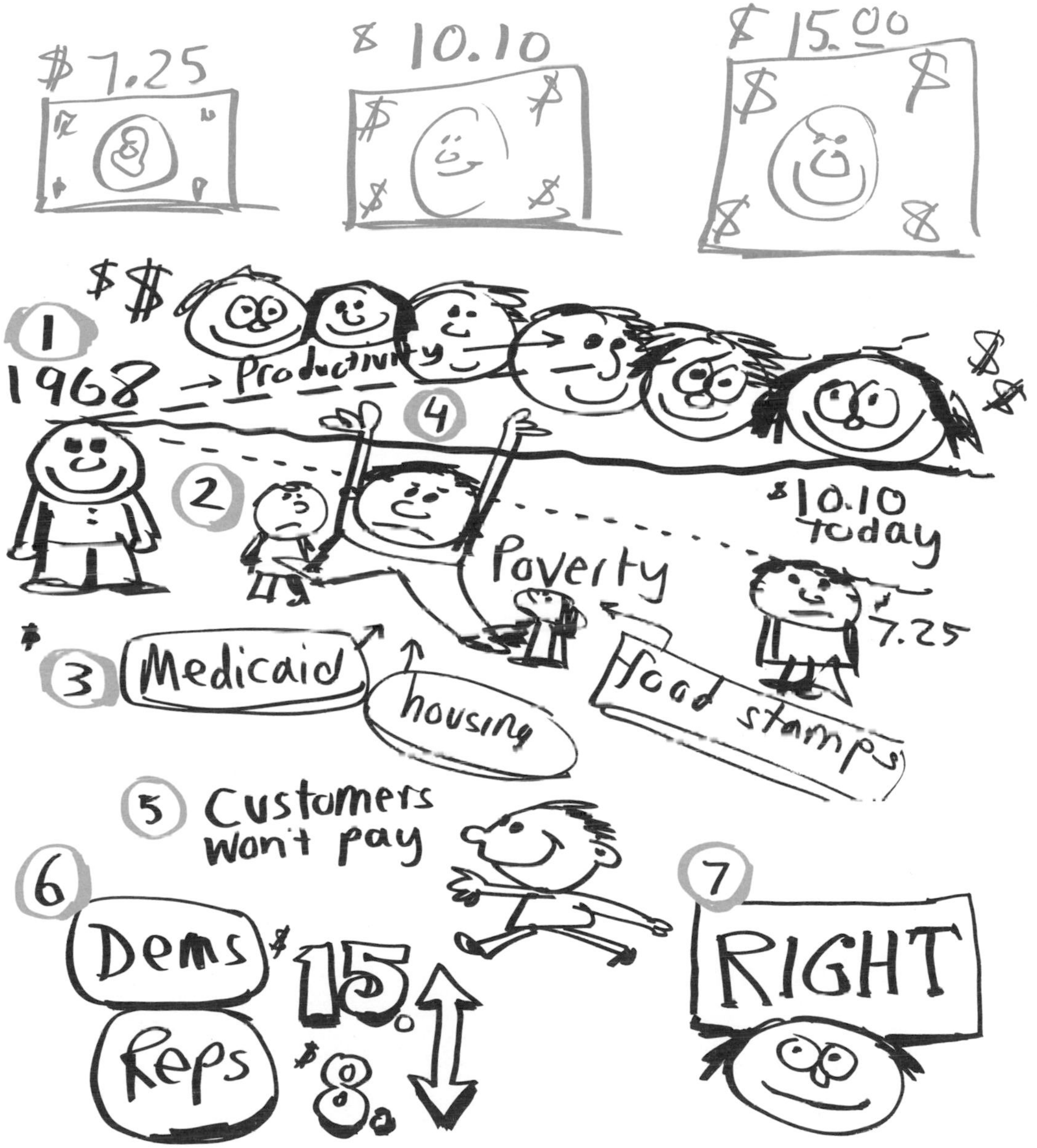
$7.25
$ 10.10
$ 15.00
$$
1
1968 → Productivity
$$
4
2
$10.10 today
Poverty
$7.25
3
Medicaid
housing
food stamps
5
Customers won't pay
6
Dems
$15.
Reps
$8.
7
RIGHT

WHY LIBERAL STATES WON AMERICA'S TAX EXPERIMENT

For years, conservatives have been telling us that a healthy business-friendly economy depends on low taxes, few regulations, and low wages. Are they right?

We've had an experiment going on here in the United States that provides an answer.

At one end of the scale are Kansas and Texas, with among the nation's lowest taxes, least regulations, and lowest wages.

At the other end is California, featuring among the nation's highest taxes (especially on the wealthy), lots of regulations (particularly when it comes to the environment), and high wages.

So according to conservative doctrine, Kansas and Texas ought to be booming, and California ought to be in the pits.

Actually, it's just the opposite. For years now, Kansas's rate of economic growth has been one of the worst in the nation. In 2015, its economy actually shrank.

Texas hasn't been doing all that much better. Its rate of job growth has been below the national average. Retail sales are way down. The value of Texas exports has been dropping.

But what about so-called over-taxed, over-regulated, high-wage California? California leads the nation in the rate of economic growth —

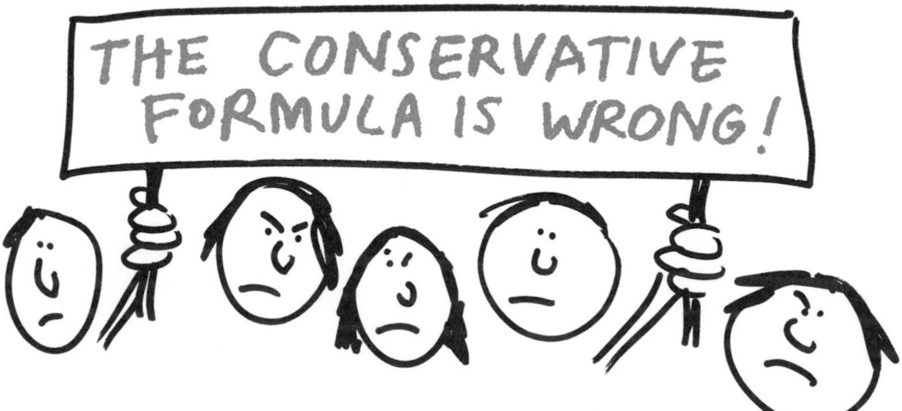
THE CONSERVATIVE FORMULA IS WRONG!

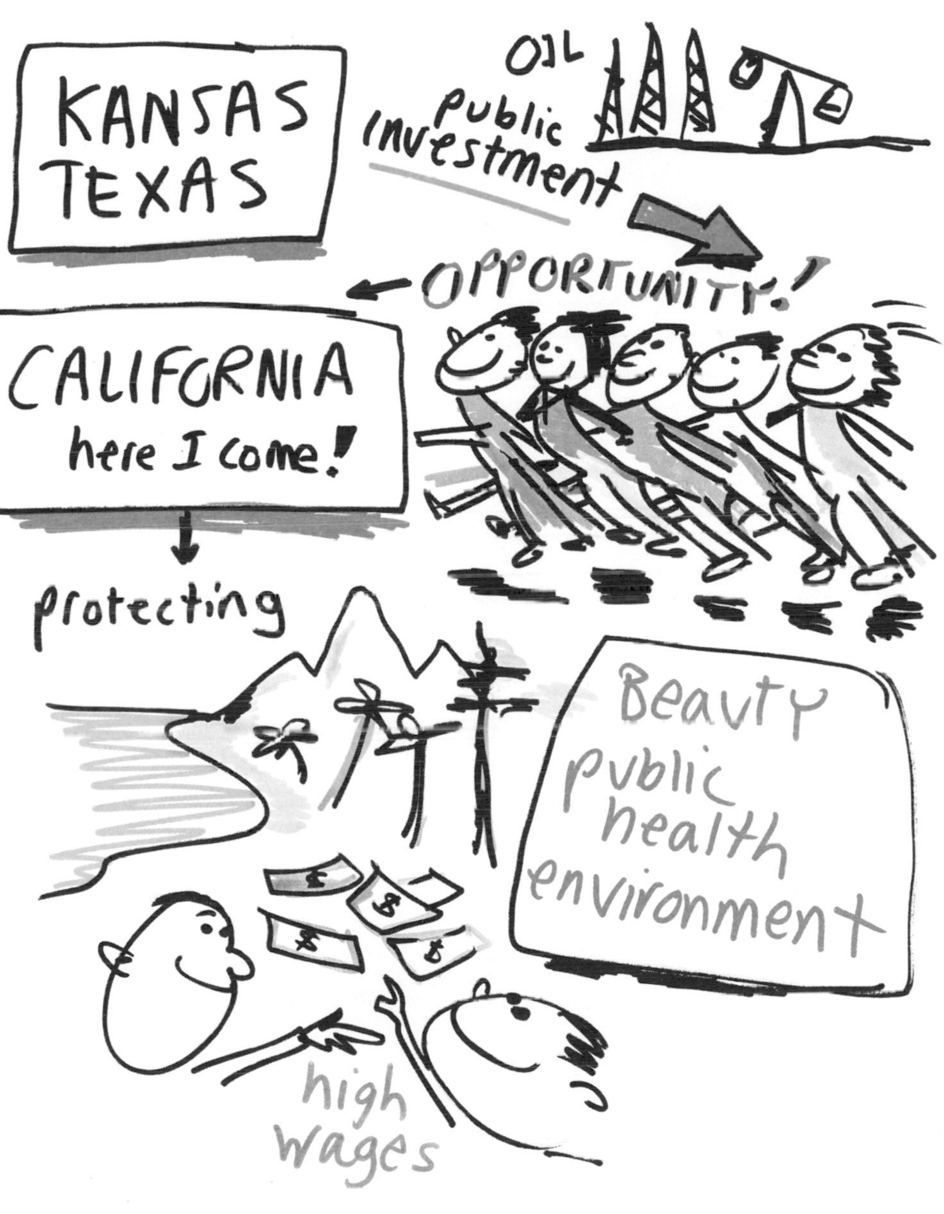
KANSAS
TEXAS
OIL
public
investment
OPPORTUNITY!
CALIFORNIA
here I come!
protecting
Beauty
public
health
environment
high
wages

more than twice the national average. In other words, conservatives have it exactly backwards.

So why are Kansas and Texas doing so badly? And why is California doing so well?

Because taxes enable states to invest in their people — education and skill training, great research universities that spawn new industries and attract talented innovators and inventors from around the globe, and modern infrastructure.

That's why California is the world center of high tech, entertainment, and venture capital.

Kansas and Texas haven't been investing nearly to the same extent.

California also provides services to a diverse population including many who are attracted to California because of its opportunities.

And California's regulations protect the public health and the state's natural beauty, which also draws people to the state — including talented people who could settle anywhere.

Wages are high in California because the economy is growing so fast employers have to pay more for workers. And that's not a bad thing. After all, the goal isn't just growth. It's a high standard of living.

Now in fairness, Texas's problems are also linked to the oil bust. But that's really no excuse because Texas has failed to diversify its economy. And here again, it hasn't made adequate investments.

California is far from perfect. A housing shortage has been driving rents and home prices into the stratosphere. And roads are clogged. Much more needs to be done.

But overall, the contrast is clear. Economic success depends on tax revenues that go into public investments, and regulations that protect the environment and public health. And true economic success results in high wages.

So the next time you hear a conservative say "low taxes, few regulations, and low wages are the keys to economic business-friendly success," just remember Kansas, Texas, and California.

The conservative formula is wrong. §

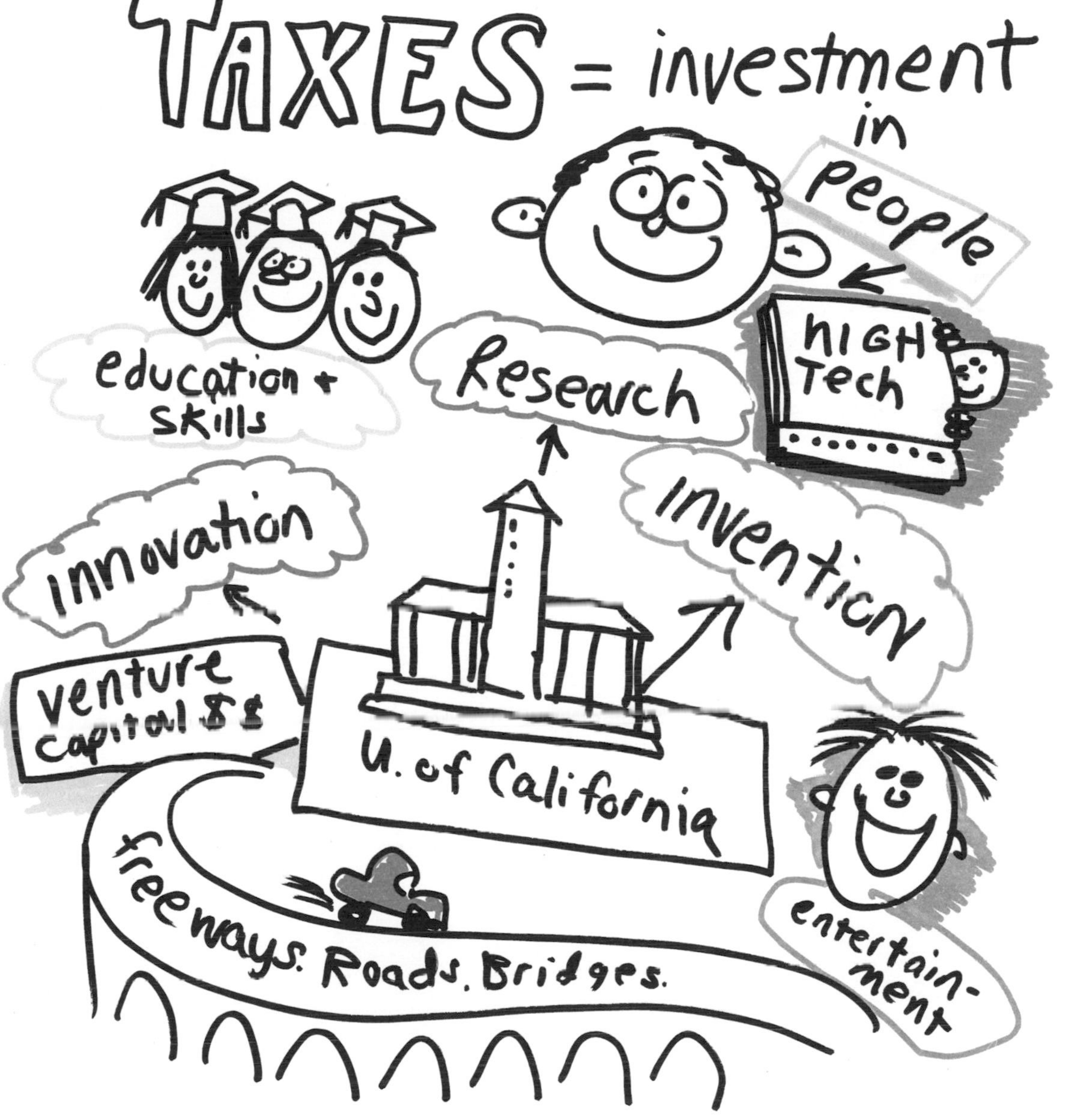
TAXES = investment in people
education + skills
Research
HIGH Tech
innovation
invention
venture capital $$
U. of California
entertainment
freeways. Roads. Bridges.

WHY THE SHARING ECONOMY IS HARMING WORKERS — AND WHAT MUST BE DONE

The so-called "sharing economy" is exploding. It includes independent contractors, free agents, temporary workers, and the self-employed. Most file 1099s rather than W2s for tax purposes. It's estimated that in five years, over 40% of the American labor force will be in such uncertain work. In a decade, most of us.

This shifts all the risks onto workers. A downturn in demand, or a sudden change in consumer needs, or a personal injury or sickness can make it impossible to pay the bills.

Gone are labor protections such as the minimum wage, worker safety, family and medical leave, and overtime. And it ends employer-financed insurance, Social Security, workers' compensation, unemployment benefits, and employer-provided health insurance.

No wonder, according to polls, almost a quarter of American workers worry they won't have enough to live on in the future. That's up from 15% a decade ago.

Such uncertainty can be hard on families, too. The children of parents who work unpredictable schedules or outside of standard daytime working hours are likely to have lower cognitive skills and more behavioral problems, according to new research.

What to do? Courts are now overflowing with lawsuits over whether companies have misclassified employees as independent contractors, resulting in a profusion of criteria and definitions.

We should aim instead for simplicity. Whoever pays more than half of somebody's income or provides more than half their working hours should be responsible for all the labor protections and insurance an employee is entitled to.

In addition, to restore some certainty to people's lives, we need to move away from unemployment insurance and toward *income* insurance. Say for example, your monthly income dips more than 50% below the average monthly income you've received from all the jobs you've taken over the preceding five years. With income insurance you'd automatically receive half the difference for up to a year.

It is possible to have a flexible economy and also provide workers some minimal level of decency and security. §

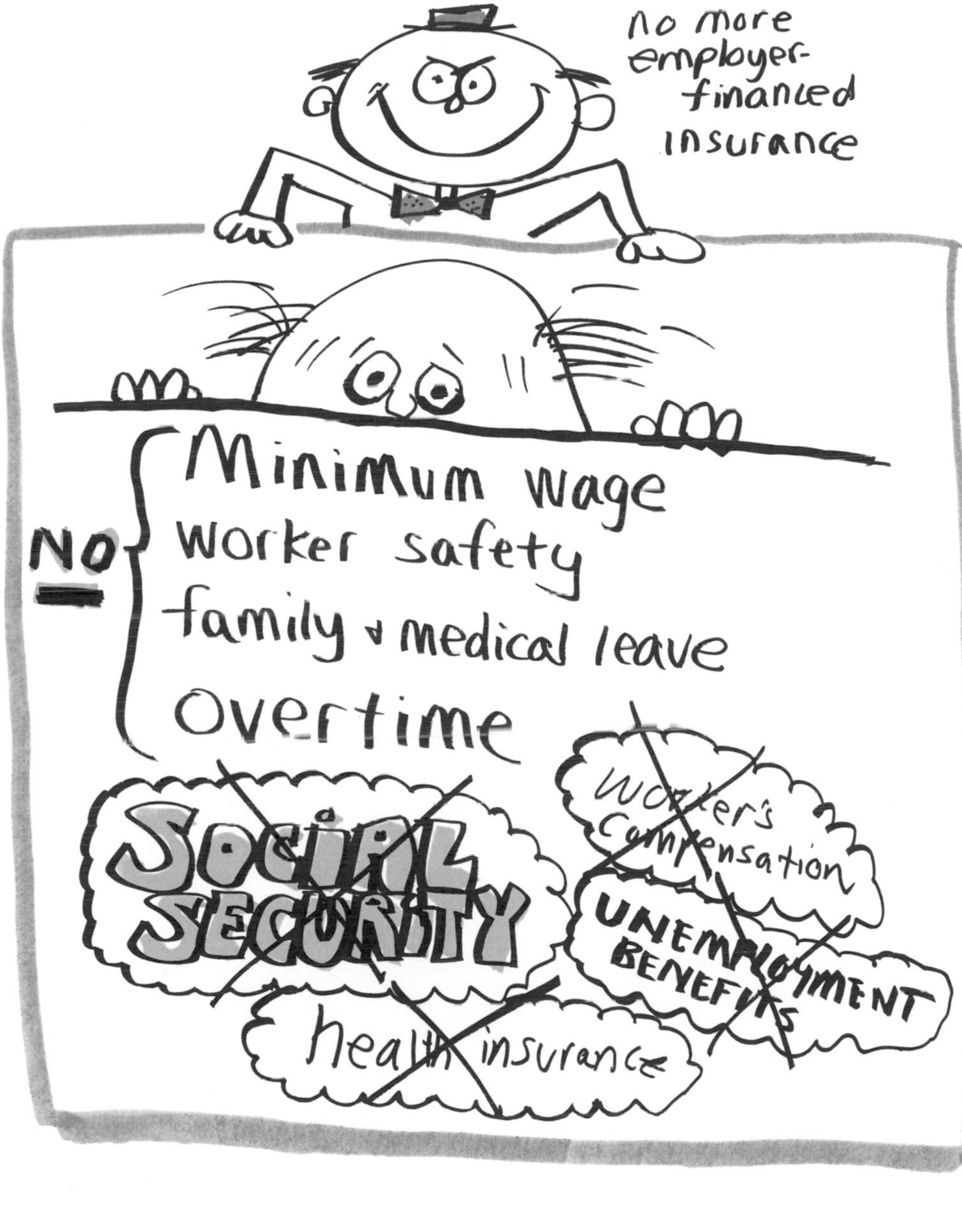
no more employer-financed insurance
NO
Minimum wage
worker safety
family + medical leave
Overtime
SOCIAL SECURITY
Worker's compensation
UNEMPLOYMENT BENEFITS
health insurance

FOUR STEPS TO SOLVING STUDENT DEBT

Do you know someone loaded down with student debt? Or do you have a big student loan? Student debt now totals $1.3 trillion, and it's growing as college costs rise faster than inflation. Faster than the incomes of most students and their families, largely because states are cutting funding to public colleges and universities where most students get their higher education.

Here are four necessary steps for dealing with the college debt crisis.

1) ALLOW GRADUATES TO REFINANCE their student loans at the same low interest rates now available to businesses and some homeowners.

2) ALLOW GRADUATES ESPECIALLY BURDENED BY STUDENT LOANS TO REORGANIZE those loans under the protection of bankruptcy. If Donald Trump can use bankruptcy to shield his fortune every time one of his businesses goes under, onerous students loans should be subject to bankruptcy too.

3) TIE FEDERAL STUDENT LOAN PAYMENTS TO HOW MUCH A GRADUATE EARNS and spread those payments out over 20 years instead of 10. That way a graduate who becomes, say, a social worker pays a far smaller amount than one who becomes an investment banker. And the payments are affordable.

4) LET'S START MOVING BACK TO THE SYSTEM WE ALMOST ACHIEVED IN THE 1950S AND 1960S — free tuition at public colleges and universities. We didn't used to think of higher education as just a private investment made by students and their families. The GI Bill, which made public college free to returning veterans, returned $7 for every $1 invested. We understood it the same way we understand K through 12: as a public good that made the nation stronger.

We shouldn't have a college debt crisis, and by taking these four steps to solve it, we all benefit. §

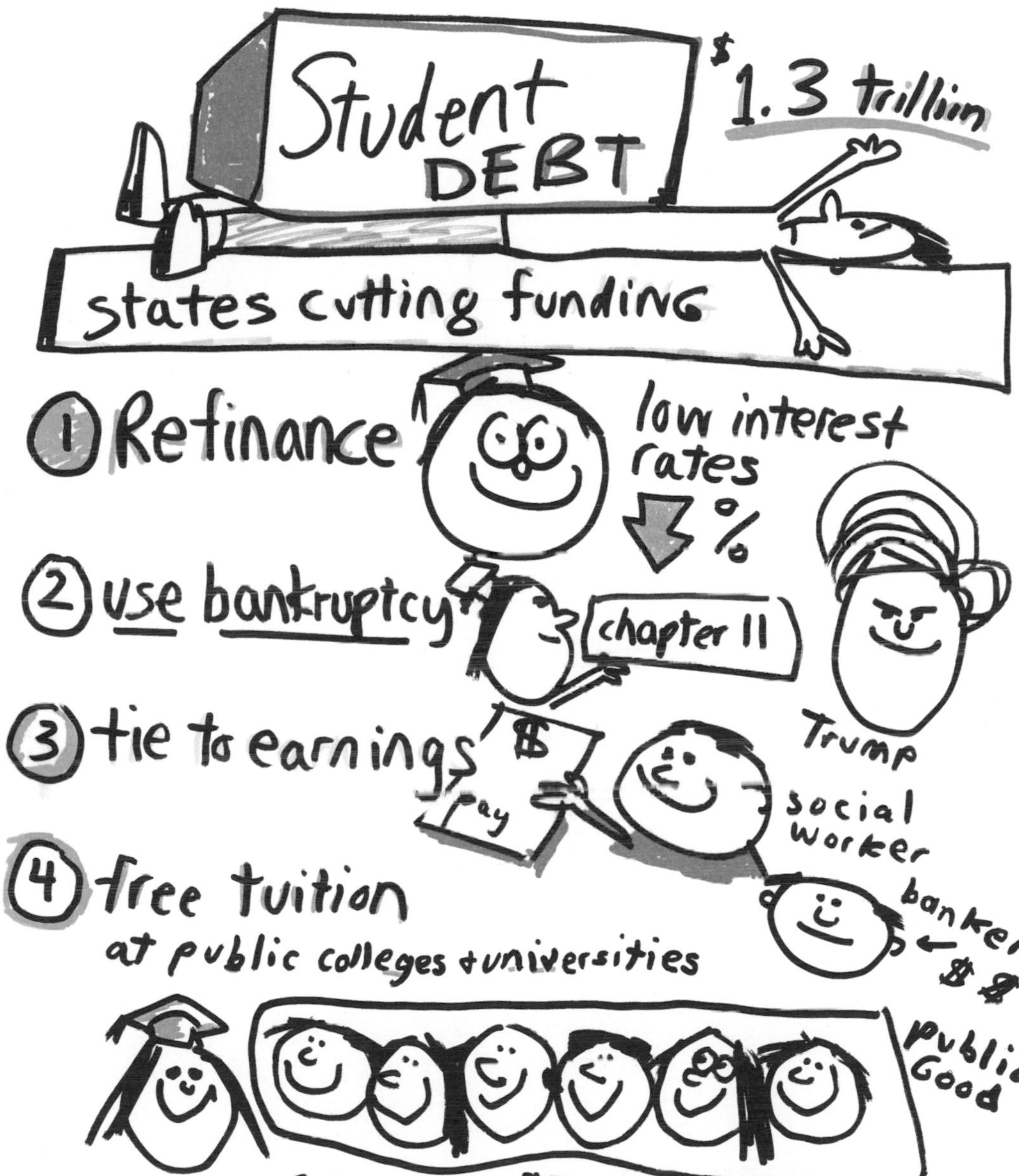
Student DEBT
$1.3 trillion
states cutting funding
1 Refinance
low interest rates
%
2 use bankruptcy
chapter 11
Trump
3 tie to earnings
$
pay
social worker
4 free tuition
at public colleges + universities
banker
$$
public Good
G.I. bill → $7 for every $1.00

WHAT IS THE RACIAL WEALTH GAP?

Why is the racial wealth gap widening? And what should be done to reverse it?

You don't hear much about the racial wealth gap, but you should. *Wealth* inequality is an even bigger problem than *income* inequality. That's because you have to have enough savings from income to begin accumulating wealth — buying a house, investing in stocks and bonds, saving to send a kid to college — but many Americans have almost no savings, so they have barely any wealth. The richest 1% of Americans own 40% of the nation's wealth. The bottom 80% own just 7%.

Low-income families of color are especially disadvantaged because they're less likely to have savings or inherit wealth. And they face significant barriers to building wealth, such as discriminatory policies that thwart home ownership.

These structural disadvantages have built up to the point where the median net worth of white families is now more than 10 times greater than that of African American and Latino families.

So, what can we do to help all Americans accumulate wealth?

1) REFORM THE TAX SYSTEM so that capital gains — that is, increases in the value of assets — are taxed at the same rate as ordinary income.

2) LIMIT HOW MUCH MORTGAGE INTEREST THE WEALTHY CAN DEDUCT from their incomes and how much retirement savings they can defer. Then use the tax savings from these changes to

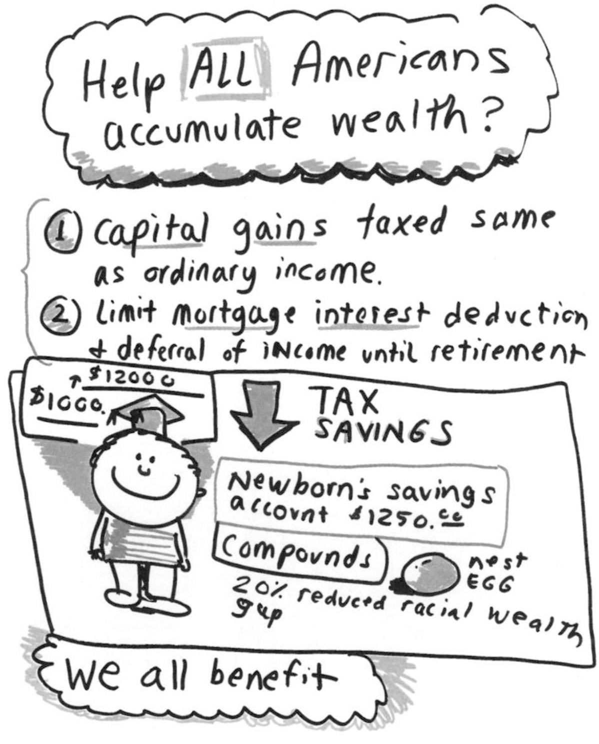

Help ALL Americans accumulate wealth?
① capital gains taxed same as ordinary income.
② Limit mortgage interest deduction + deferral of income until retirement
$12000
$1000.
TAX SAVINGS
Newborn's savings account $1250.00
Compounds
nest EGG
20% reduced racial wealth gap
We all benefit

help lower-income people gain a foothold in building their own wealth.

For example, provide every newborn child with a savings account of at least $1,250 — more if a child is from a low-income family. This sum will compound over the years into a solid nest egg. Research shows that this policy alone could reduce the racial wealth gap by nearly 20%.

At age 18, that young person could use the money for tuition or training, a business, or a home. Studies show such accounts can change children's behavior and increase the likelihood they'll attend college.

3) ALLOW FAMILIES RECEIVING PUBLIC BENEFITS TO SAVE. Today, a family receiving public assistance can be cut off for having saved just $1,000.

Raise the limits to what a family can save to at least $12,000 — roughly three months' income for a low-income family of four — and thereby put that family on the road to self-sufficiency.

These simple steps will allow families to invest in their own futures, which is the surest way out of poverty.

All of us benefit when everyone has the opportunity to accumulate wealth. §

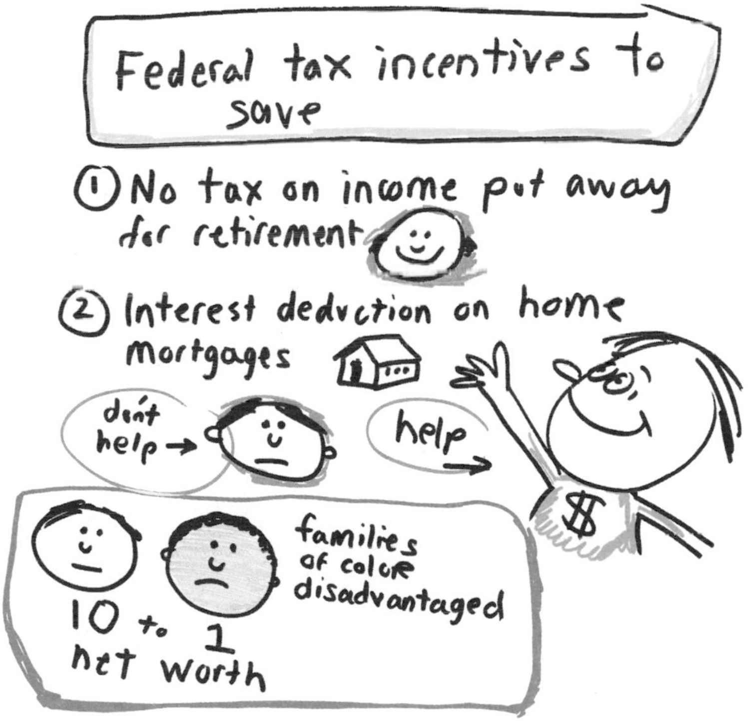
Federal tax incentives to save
① No tax on income put away for retirement
② Interest deduction on home mortgages
don't help →
help →
$
families of color disadvantaged
10 to 1 net worth

THE WOMEN'S WEALTH GAP

A conversation between Robert Reich and Elena Chavez Quezada, co-founder of Closing The Women's Wealth Gap Initiative

ROBERT REICH: It's been a while since millions of women marching in cities across the U.S. focused our attention on gender inequality. One issue that caught my attention is the fact that women are more likely to be the sole, primary, or co-breadwinner in their families than ever before, yet they still earn far less than men.

ELENA CHAVEZ QUEZADA: Income inequality is a key issue affecting the economic security of women and their families. But even if we closed the *pay* gap, a yawning *wealth* gap would remain. We all know women earn 79 cents for every dollar earned by men, but most people don't realize that women own only 32 cents on the dollar; and black and Latina women own just pennies on the dollar compared to white men and white women. So — if we're going to build women's economic security, we have to tackle income *and* wealth inequality.

BOB: How is wealth different than income? And why is the wealth gap between women and men so large?

ELENA: Wealth is a much more accurate description of how you're doing financially. It's a balance of assets minus debts.

Several factors contribute to the women's wealth gap. To name a few:

Wealth gap
$1.00
own
32¢
compared to men
black + latina women just pennies
compared to white men (+ women)

WEALTH
vs. income
Total assets
minus
debts
savings
car
home
$
earn less
→
+
part-time
+ tax subsidies not available
Women of color especially impacted

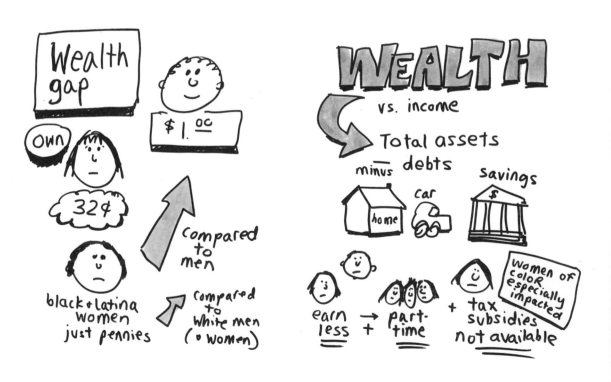

Women make less than men so we're less able to save. We're more likely to work part-time, usually because we're caring for family members, which limits our access to employer benefits that help turn income into wealth.

We often can't access tax subsidies that encourage savings and investment, for retirement or home ownership, because of the way they're structured.

And all of these challenges are more intense for women of color who are impacted by racial and gender disparities.

BOB: So what can we do about it?

ELENA: We need a broad menu of solutions that addresses income and wealth inequality.

On the income side, we need to keep pushing for pay equity, affordable childcare, and paid family leave.

On the wealth side, we could start by tackling two key challenges — retirement savings and tax benefits.

FIRST, WE NEED TO SUPPORT NEW STRATEGIES TO EXPAND WOMEN'S ACCESS TO RETIREMENT ACCOUNTS — like state programs such as Secure Choice in California, for example — that enable smaller employers to offer their workers access to accounts; and "portable benefits" — tied to individuals, not employers — so independent contractors, domestic workers, and Lyft drivers can access them.

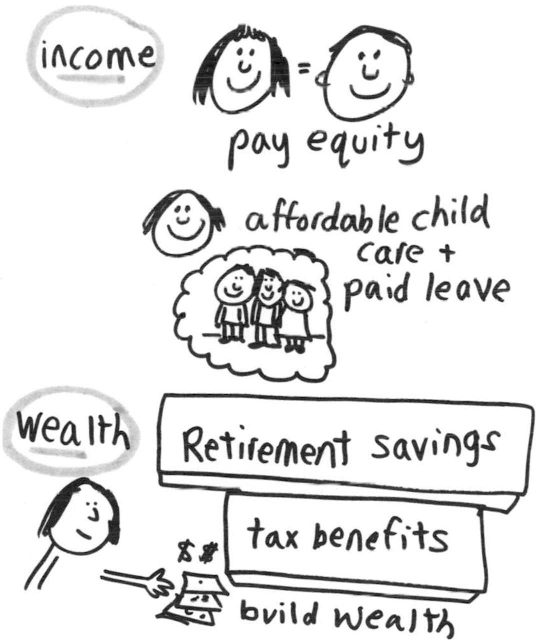
income
pay equity
affordable child care +
paid leave
wealth
Retirement savings
tax benefits
$$
build wealth

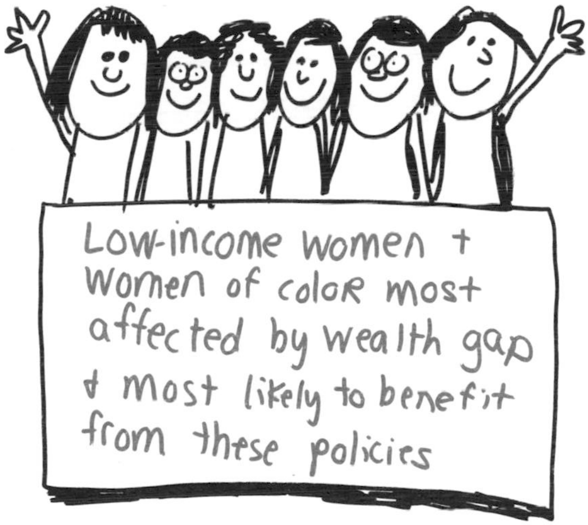
Low-income women + women of color most affected by wealth gap + most likely to benefit from these policies

SECOND, WE NEED TO KEEP ASKING "WHO BENEFITS?" as policymakers debate tax reform. If working women and their families don't benefit, we need to push back. For example:

Two-thirds of households — and most of those led by working women — don't itemize on their taxes, so they don't benefit from deductions, like the home mortgage tax credit.

Working families and households led by women are much more likely to benefit from tax credits, especially if they're refundable. Expanding the Earned Income Tax Credit and the Child Tax Credit should be key priorities for women.

These strategies support everyone; but they would really benefit low-income women and women of color, who are most affected by the women's wealth gap.

BOB: So closing the women's wealth gap is good for families, communities, and the national economy. It gives families the cushion they need to weather a financial crisis. It helps them save and invest in their communities.

And all of these strategies contribute to a strong economy.

In short — we all benefit. §

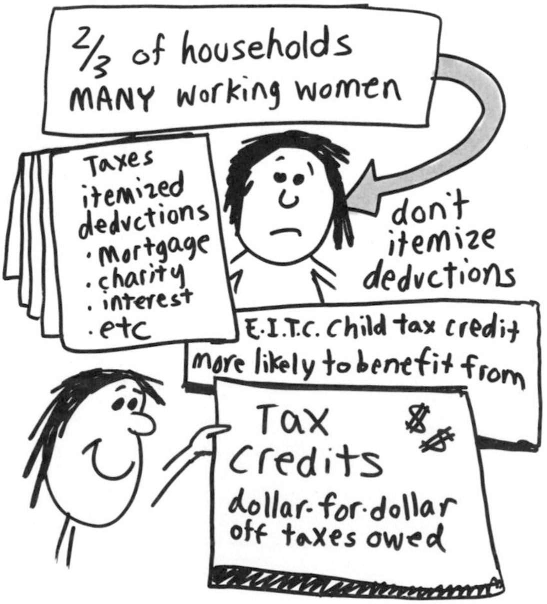

2/3 of households
MANY working women
Taxes
itemized
deductions
· Mortgage
· charity
· interest
· etc
don't
itemize
deductions
E.I.T.C. Child tax credit
more likely to benefit from
Tax
credits
$
$
dollar-for-dollar
off taxes owed

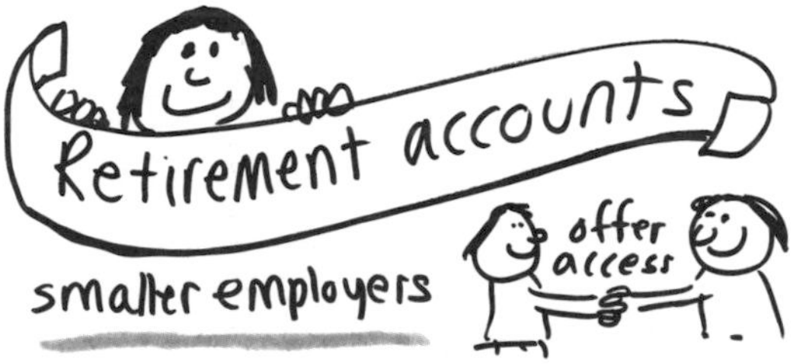

Retirement accounts
smaller employers
offer
access

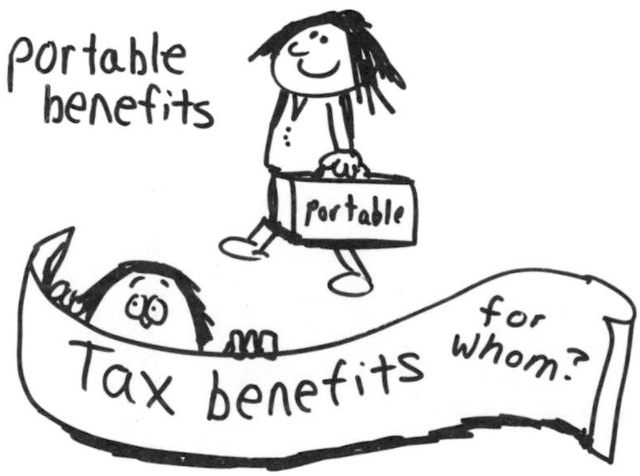

portable
benefits
Portable
Tax benefits
for
Whom?

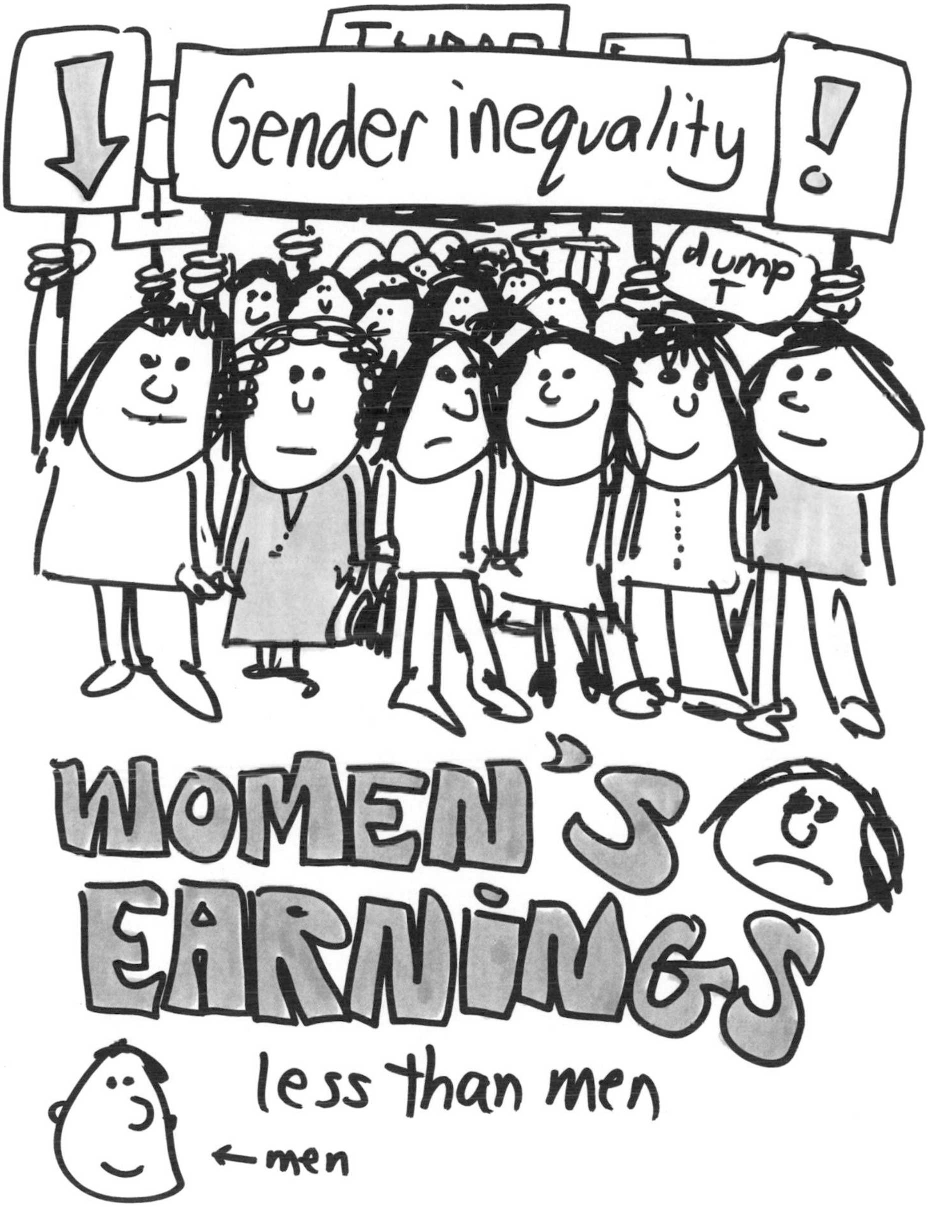
Gender inequality
dump T
WOMEN'S EARNINGS
less than men
← men

END MASS INCARCERATION NOW

We need to end mass incarceration now. Imprisoning large numbers of Americans is wrong. It's also racist. A person of color is more likely to be stopped by the police, questioned, and arrested even if they've done exactly the same thing that I, a white man, have done. He or she is more likely to be convicted and sent to jail.

It's also bad for the economy. In the big picture, today the United States has 5% of the world's population but 25% of its prisoners, and we spend more than $80 billion each year on prisons. There were fewer than 200,000 Americans behind bars as recently as the mid-1970s, but mandatory minimums and "three-strikes-you're-out" laws ballooned that number to nearly two-and-a-half million today, despite widespread evidence that locking people up doesn't make us any safer.

Even though blacks, whites, and Latinos use drugs at similar rates, people with black and brown skin are more likely to be pulled over, searched, arrested, charged with a crime, convicted, and imprisoned.

Here's how the economy also pays a huge price. A felony conviction can bar people from getting a student loan, a mortgage, even from voting. It might also disqualify them from getting a job. All of this means a lot of potential human talent is going to waste. We're spending a fortune locking people up who could fuel our economy and build strong communities.

So what to do?

1) ENACT SMARTER SENTENCING LAWS, end mandatory minimums, and transform the way we treat people who enter the criminal justice system. Instead of just prisons and jails, we need cost-effective alternatives to incarceration — like job training, mental-health support, and drug-treatment programs.

2) STOP MILITARIZING THE POLICE. And end discriminatory policing practices such as "stop-and-frisk" and "broken windows" in target communities of color.

3) STOP BUILDING NEW JAILS. And close some existing ones. States are spending more and more on prisons while cutting funding for schools. That's nuts.

4) BAN THE "BOX." Stop asking on job applications whether you've ever been convicted of a felony. Already, dozens of states, cities, and counties have passed bills demanding that employers consider what you can do in the future, not what you might have done in the past.

Instead of locking people up unjustly and then locking them out of the economy for the rest of their lives, we need to stop wasting human talent and start opening doors of opportunity to everyone. §

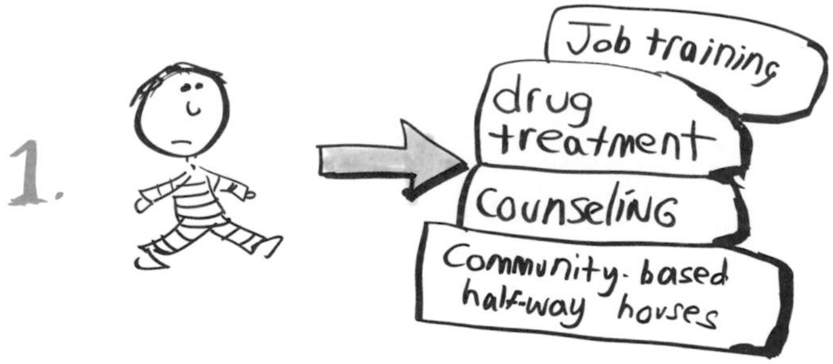
1.
Job training
drug treatment
Counseling
Community-based half-way houses

2.

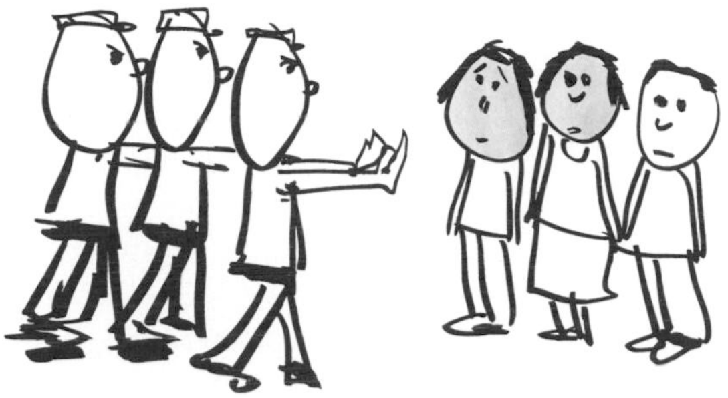

3.

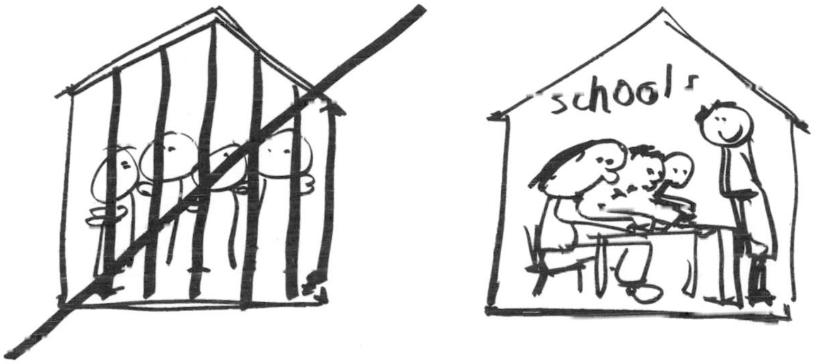
schools

4.

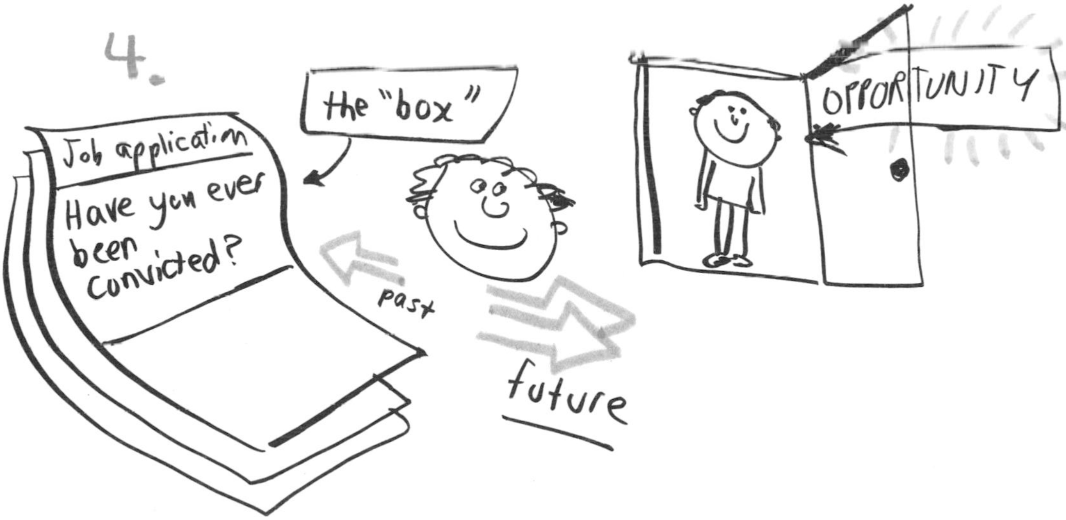
the "box"
Job application
Have you ever been convicted?
past
future
OPPORTUNITY

WHY A TAX ON WALL STREET TRADES IS AN EVEN BETTER IDEA THAN YOU KNOW

One of Bernie Sanders's most important proposals didn't receive enough attention, but it should become law — it's a tax on financial transactions.

THE ARGUMENTS FOR IT

Putting a small tax on financial transactions would:

1) REDUCE INCENTIVES FOR HIGH SPEED TRADING, INSIDER DEALMAKING, AND SHORT-TERM FINANCIAL BETTING. Buying and selling stocks and bonds in order to beat others who are buying stocks and bonds is a giant zero-sum game. It wastes countless resources, uses up the talents of some of the nation's best and brightest, and subjects financial markets to unnecessary risk.

2) GENERATE LOTS OF REVENUE. Even a 1/10 of 1% transaction tax would raise $185 billion over 10 years, according to the non-partisan Tax Policy Center. It could thereby finance public investments that enlarge the economic pie rather than merely rearranging its slices — investments like better schools and access to college.

3) BE FAIR. Americans pay sales taxes on all sorts of goods and services, yet Wall Street traders pay no sales tax on the stocks and bonds they buy — which helps explain why the financial industry generates about 30% of all of America's corporate profits, but pays only about 18% of corporate taxes.

THE ARGUMENTS AGAINST IT

According to Wall Street, even a small tax on financial transactions would:

1) DRIVE TRADING OVERSEAS, since trades can easily be done elsewhere.

Baloney. The U.K. has had a tax on stock trades for decades, yet remains one of the world's financial powerhouses. Incidentally, that tax raises about three billion pounds yearly, which is a big help for Britain's budget. (That's the equivalent of $30 billion in an economy the size of the United States.) At least 40 other countries also have such a tax, and the European Union is on the way to implementing one.

2) UNDULY BURDEN SMALL INVESTORS such as retirees, business owners, and average savers.

Wrong again. The tax wouldn't be a burden if it reduces the volume and frequency of trading, which is the whole point. In fact, the tax is highly progressive. The Tax Policy Center estimates that 75% of it would be paid by the richest 1/5 of taxpayers and 40% by the top 1%.

SO WHY AREN'T POLITICIANS OF ALL STRIPES SUPPORTING A TAX ON FINANCIAL TRANSACTIONS?

Because the financial transactions tax directly threatens a major source of Wall Street's revenue. And if you hadn't noticed, the Street uses a portion of its vast revenues to gain political clout — which may be the best reason for enacting it. §

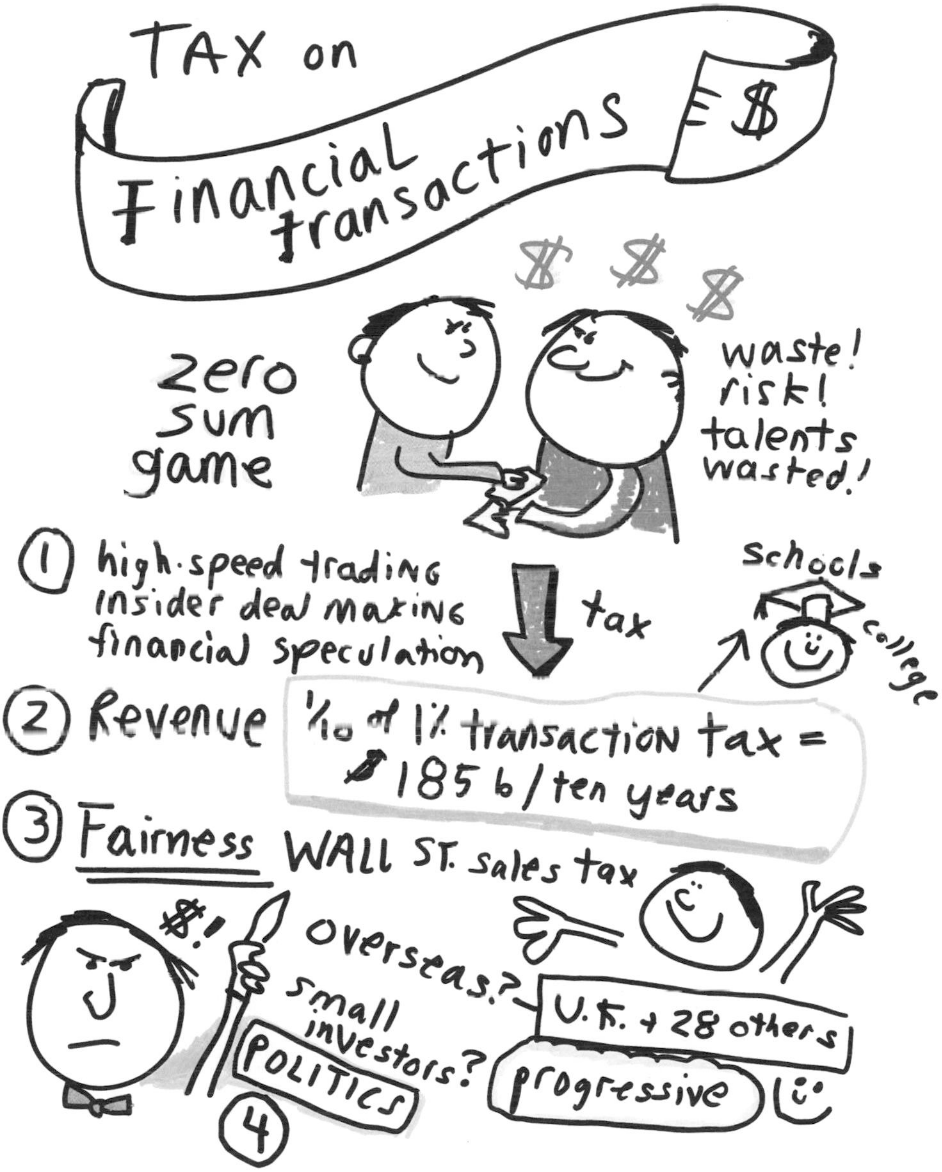

TAX on
Financial transactions
$
$ $ $
zero sum game
waste! risk! talents wasted!
① high-speed trading
insider deal making
financial speculation
tax
schools
college
② Revenue
1/10 of 1% transaction tax =
$185 b/ten years
③ Fairness WALL ST. sales tax
$!
overseas?
U.K. + 28 others
small investors?
POLITICS
④
progressive

WHY WE'LL NEED A UNIVERSAL BASIC INCOME

Imagine a little gadget called an iEverything. You can't get it yet, but if technology keeps moving as fast as it is now, the iEverything will be with us before you know it.

A combination of intelligent computing, 3-D manufacturing, big data crunching, and advanced biotechnology, this little machine will be able to do everything you want and give you everything you need.

There's only one hitch. As the economy is now organized, no one will be able to buy it, because there won't be any paying jobs left. You see, the iEverything will do … everything.

I exaggerate to make a point, but we're heading toward something like the iEverything far quicker than most people realize. Even now, we're producing more and more goods and services with fewer and fewer people. Internet sales are

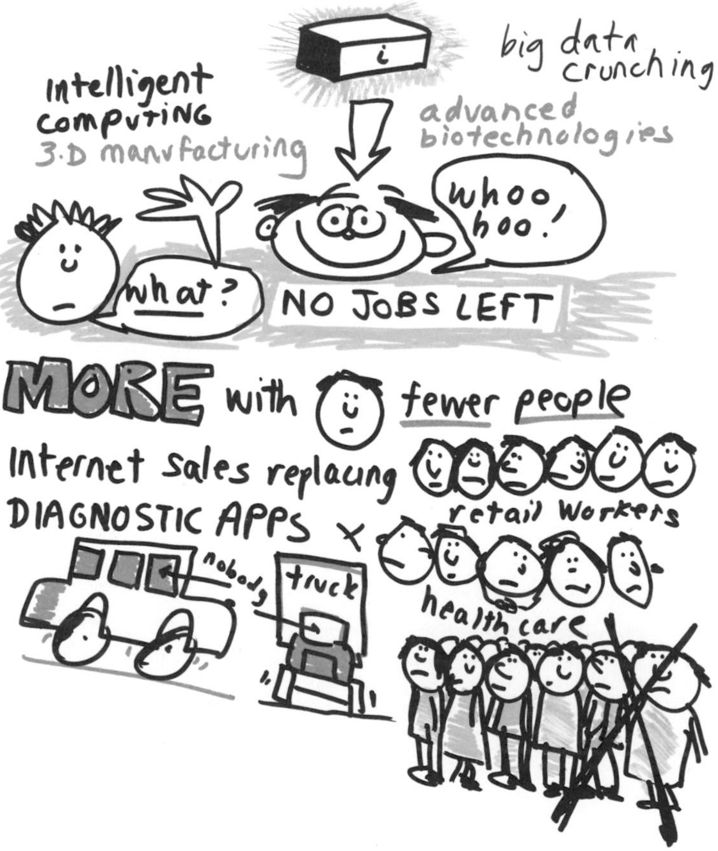

i
big data crunching
intelligent computing
3-D manufacturing
advanced biotechnologies
whoo, hoo!
what?
NO JOBS LEFT
MORE with fewer people
internet sales replacing
retail workers
DIAGNOSTIC APPS
nobody
truck
health care

on the way to replacing millions of retail workers. Diagnostic apps will be replacing hundreds of thousands of healthcare workers. Self-driving cars and trucks will replace five million drivers. Researchers estimate that almost half of all U.S. jobs are at risk of being automated in the next two decades.

This isn't necessarily bad. The economy we're heading toward could offer millions of people more free time to do what they want to do instead of what they have to do to earn a living.

But to make this work, we'll have to figure out some way to recirculate the money from the relatively few people who will do very well in the economy of the iEverything to the rest of us who will want to buy iEverythings.

One answer worth serious consideration: A universal basic income — possibly financed

free time!

owners of labor-replacing technologies

the rest of us

recirculate the $ $ $

Universal BASIC INCOME

out of the profits flowing to labor-replacing innovations.

The idea of a universal basic income isn't as radical as it may sound. Historically, it's had support from people on both the left and the right. In the 1970s, President Nixon proposed a similar concept for the United States, and it even passed the House of Representatives.

The idea is getting some traction again, partly because of the speed of technological change. I keep running into executives of high-tech companies who tell me a universal basic income is inevitable, eventually.

Some conservatives believe it's superior to welfare or other kinds of public assistance, because a universal basic income doesn't tell peo-

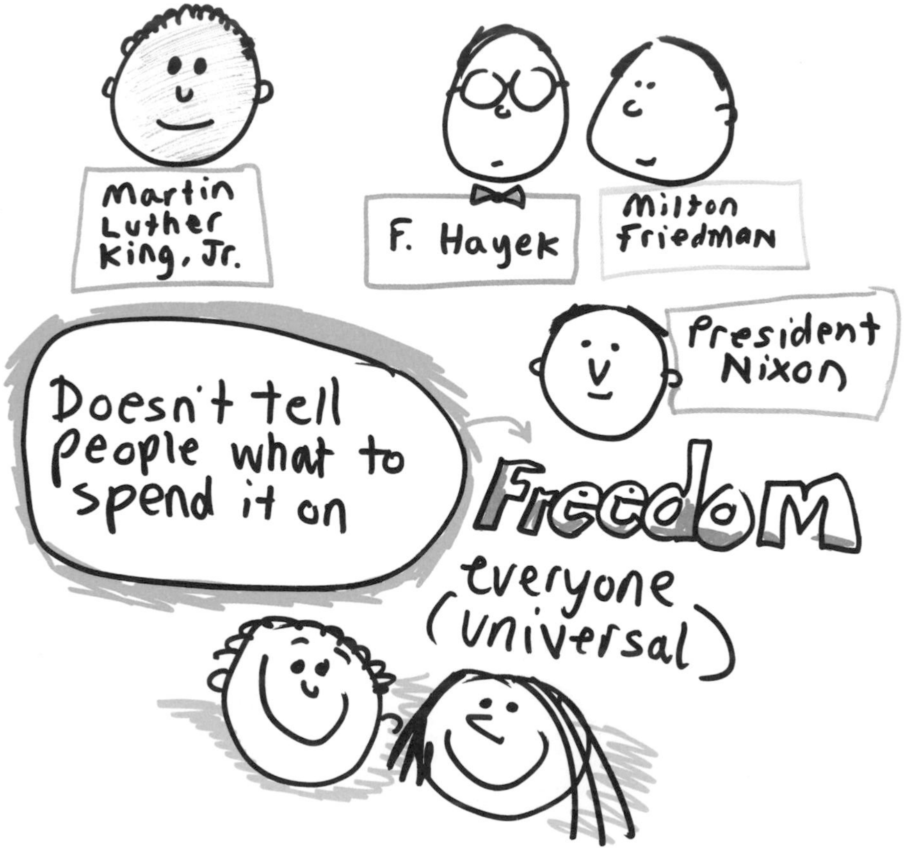

Martin Luther King, Jr.
F. Hayek
Milton Friedman
President Nixon
Doesn't tell people what to spend it on
Freedom
everyone (universal)

ple what to spend the assistance on. Nor does it stigmatize recipients, because everyone qualifies.

In recent years, evidence has shown that giving people cash as a way to address poverty actually works. In study after study, people don't stop working, and they don't drink it away. They actually use it to increase their earnings.

Interest in a basic income is surging, with governments debating it from Finland to Canada to Switzerland to Namibia. The charity Give Directly is about to launch a basic income pilot in Kenya, providing an income for 12 years to some of the poorest, most vulnerable families on the planet. And then rigorously evaluate the results.

As new technologies replace work, the question is how best to provide economic security for all. A universal basic income will almost certainly be part of the answer. §

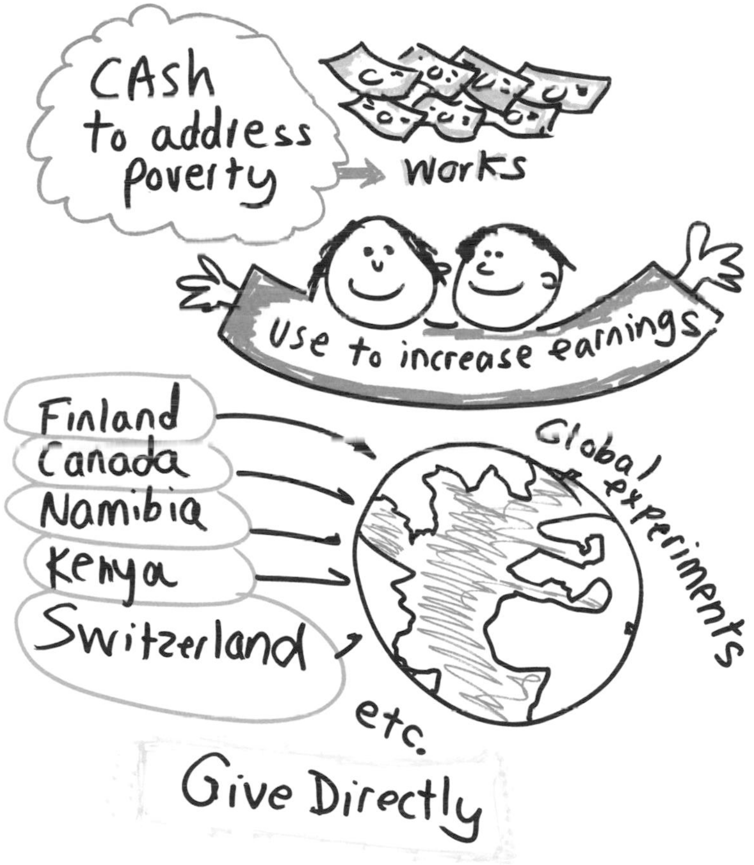

CASh to address poverty
works
Use to increase earnings
Finland
Canada
Namibia
Kenya
Switzerland
Global experiments
etc.
Give Directly

BERNIE SANDERS'S SEVEN LEGACIES

The movement Senator Bernie Sanders began during the 2016 Democratic primary campaign is still just beginning. He's provided it with seven big legacies.

1) BERNIE HELPED OPEN AMERICA'S EYES TO THE BIG MONEY CORRUPTING OUR DEMOCRACY — and thereby rigging our economy to its advantage and everyone else's disadvantage. Polls now show huge majorities of Americans think moneyed interests have too much sway in Washington.

2) BERNIE SHOWED THAT IT'S POSSIBLE TO WIN ELECTIONS WITHOUT DEPENDING ON BIG MONEY from corporations, Wall Street, and billionaires. He came close to winning the Democratic nomination on the basis of millions of small donations from average working people. No longer can a

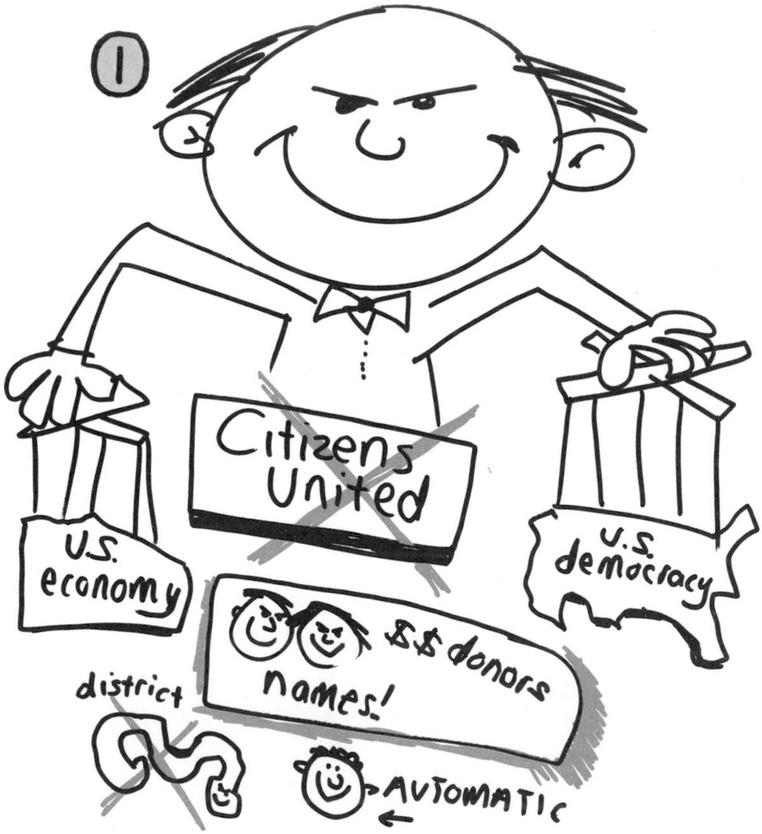
1
Citizens United
U.S. economy
U.S. democracy
$$ donors
names!
district
AUTOMATIC

candidate pretend to believe in campaign finance reform but say they have to take big money because their opponent does.

3) BERNIE EDUCATED MILLIONS OF AMERICANS ABOUT WHY WE MUST HAVE A SINGLE-PAYER HEALTHCARE SYSTEM, free tuition at public universities, why we must resurrect the Glass-Steagall Act, and why we must bust up the biggest banks. These issues will be front and center in every progressive campaign from now on, at all levels of American politics.

4) BERNIE'S CAMPAIGN HAS BROUGHT MILLIONS OF YOUNG PEOPLE INTO POLITICS, unleashing their energy and enthusiasm and idealism.

5) BERNIE IGNITED A MOVEMENT TO PUSH THE DEMOCRATIC PARTY to take more progressive posi-

2
small donors
small donors
Democracy
I have to take big money because my opponent does.

3
Single payer ℞
free tuition at public univs.
Glass.Steagall
Bust biggest banks
$

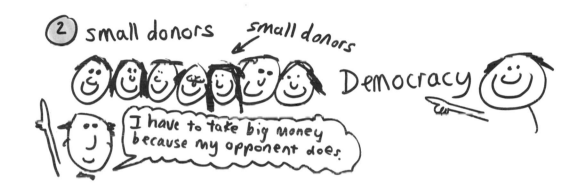

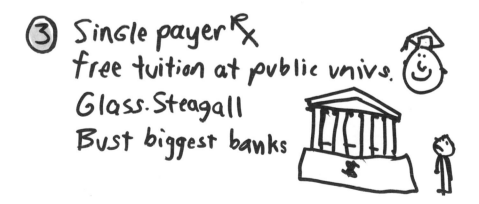

tions on issues such as the minimum wage, Wall Street, and Social Security.

6) BERNIE TAUGHT AMERICANS HOW UNDEMOCRATIC THE DEMOCRATIC PARTY'S SYSTEM FOR PICKING CANDIDATES REALLY IS. Before Bernie, not many paid attention to the so-called "superdelegates," or whether independents could vote, or how primary elections and caucuses were really run. From now on, people will pay attention. And the Democratic National Committee will be under pressure to make fundamental changes.

7) BERNIE HAS SPOTLIGHTED THE REAL POSSIBILITY THAT IF THE DEMOCRATIC PARTY DOES NOT

a) respond to the necessity of getting big money out of politics
b) commit to reversing widening inequality
c) begin to advocate for a single-payer healthcare system

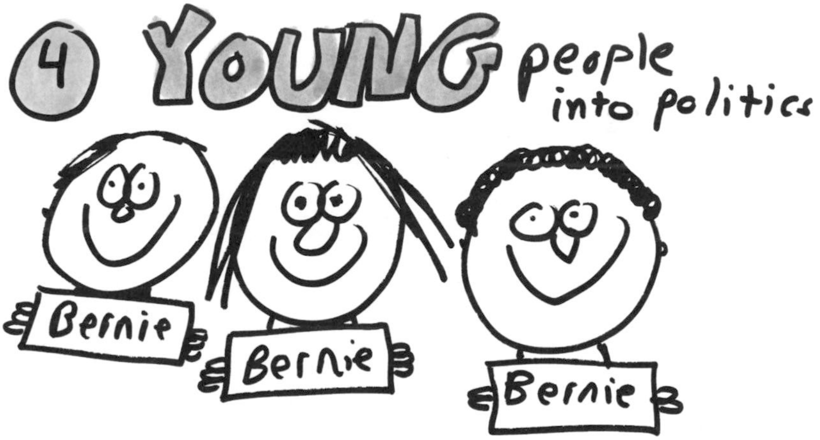
4
YOUNG people into politics
Bernie
Bernie
Bernie

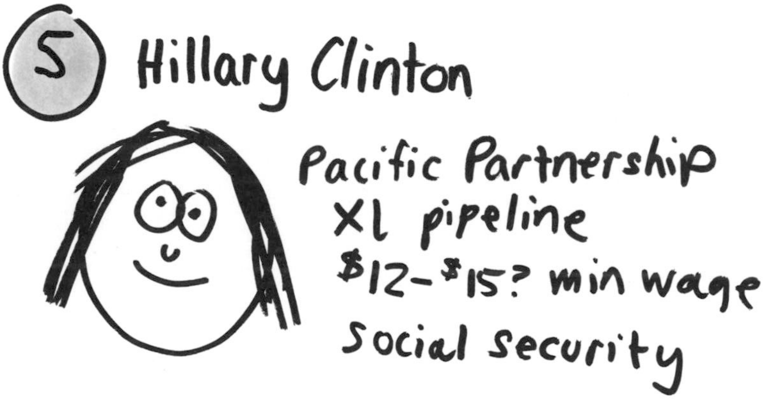
5
Hillary Clinton
Pacific Partnership
XL pipeline
$12-$15? min wage
Social Security

d) push hard for higher taxes on the wealthy — including a wealth tax — to pay for better education and better opportunities for everyone else
e) expand Social Security and lift the cap on income subject to the Social Security payroll tax
f) bust up the biggest banks and strengthen antitrust laws, and
g) expand voting rights

— then the Democratic Party will become irrelevant to the future of America.

Bernie, we thank you for your courage, your inspiration, your tireless dedication, and your vision.

And we will continue the fight. §

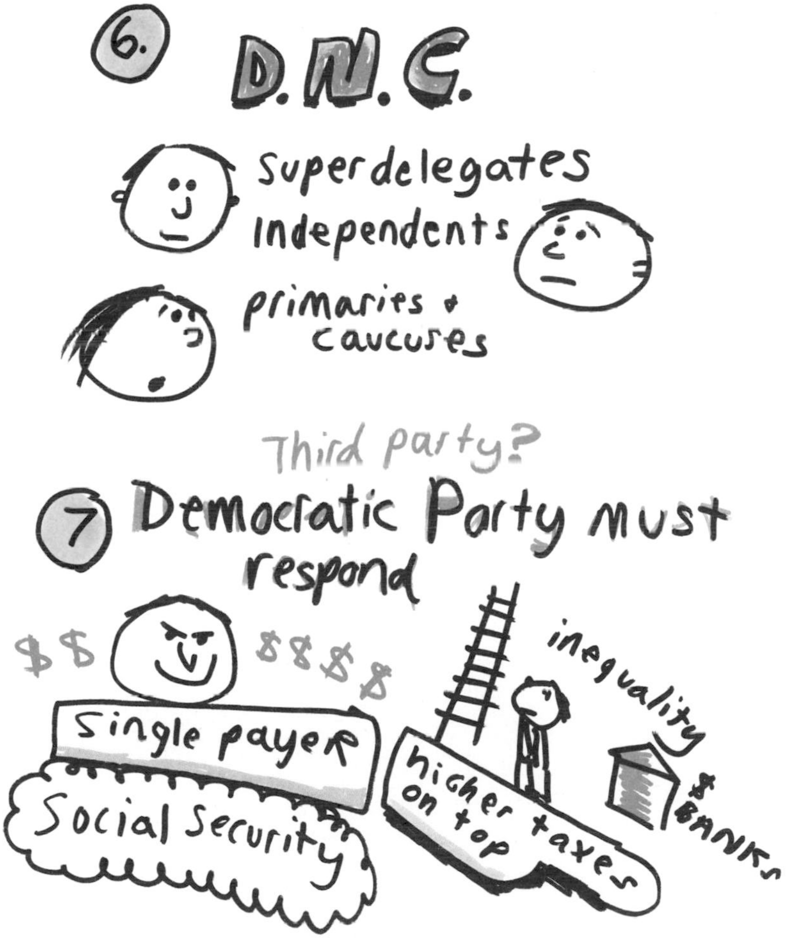

6.
D.N.C.
superdelegates
independents
primaries &
caucuses
Third party?
7
Democratic Party must respond
$$
$$$$
single payer
Social Security
higher taxes on top
inequality
$ BANKS

TRUMPONOMICS

SEVEN SIGNS OF TYRANNY

As tyrants take control of democracies, they typically do seven things:

1) **THEY EXAGGERATE THEIR MANDATE TO GOVERN** — claiming, for example, that they won an election by a "landslide" even after losing the popular vote. They criticize any finding that they or co-conspirators stole the election. And they claim "massive voter fraud" in the absence of any evidence, in order to have an excuse to restrict voting by opponents in subsequent elections.

2) **THEY TURN THE PUBLIC AGAINST JOURNALISTS AND MEDIA OUTLETS THAT CRITICIZE THEM,** calling them "deceitful" and "scum," and telling the public that the press is a "public enemy." They hold few, if any, press conferences, and prefer to communicate directly through mass rallies and unfiltered statements (such as tweets).

3) **THEY REPEATEDLY LIE TO THE PUBLIC, EVEN WHEN CONFRONTED WITH THE FACTS.** Repeated enough, these lies cause some of the public to doubt the truth, and to believe fictions that support the tyrants' goals.

4) **THEY BLAME ECONOMIC STRESSES ON IMMIGRANTS OR RACIAL OR RELIGIOUS MINORITIES,** and foment public bias or even violence against those groups. They threaten mass deportations, "registries" of religious minorities, and the banning of refugees.

5) **THEY ATTACK THE MOTIVES OF ANYONE WHO OPPOSES THEM, INCLUDING JUDGES.** They attribute acts of domestic violence to "enemies within," and use such events as excuses to beef up internal security and limit civil liberties.

6) **THEY APPOINT FAMILY MEMBERS TO HIGH POSITIONS OF AUTHORITY.** They appoint their own personal security force rather than a security detail accountable to the public. And they put generals into top civilian posts.

7) **THEY KEEP THEIR PERSONAL FINANCES SECRET, AND DRAW NO DISTINCTION BETWEEN PERSONAL PROPERTY AND PUBLIC PROPERTY** — profiteering from their public office.

Consider yourself warned. §

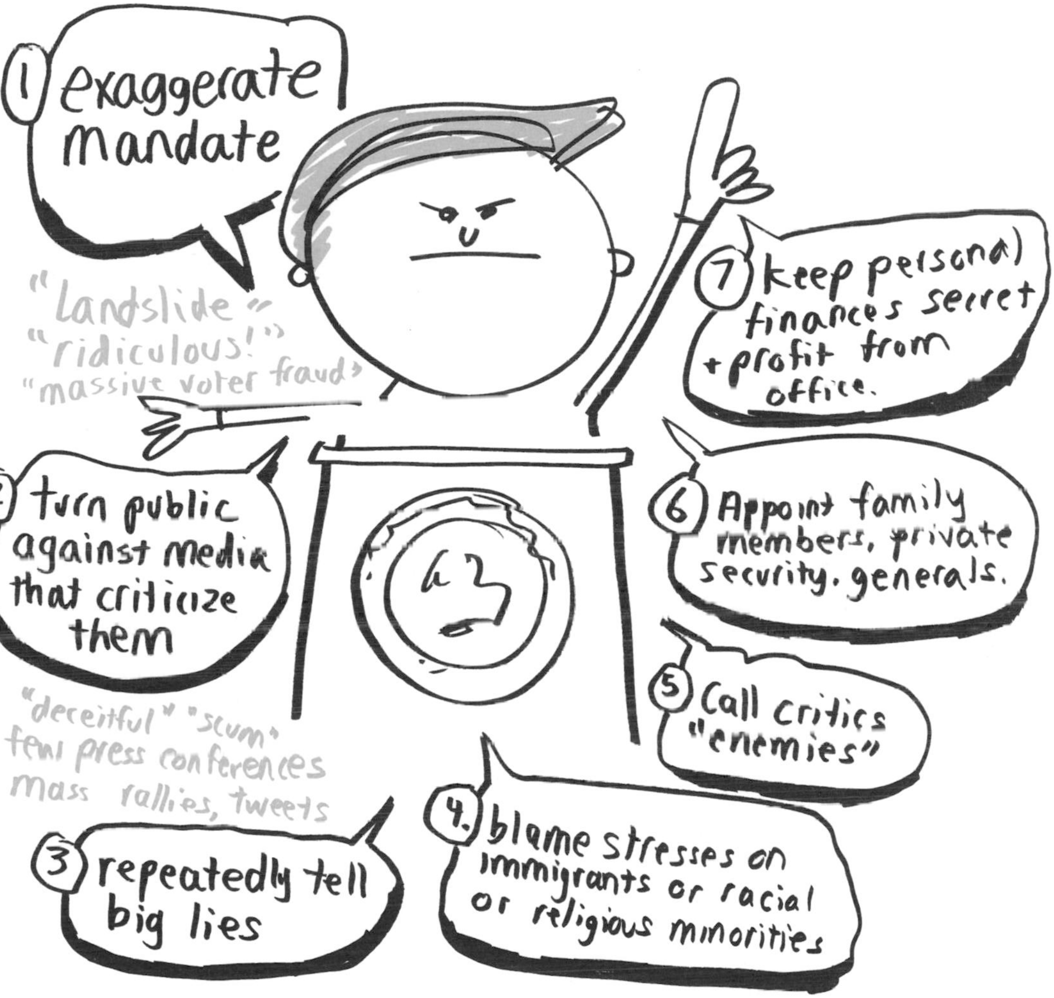

1 exaggerate mandate
"landslide"
"ridiculous!"
"massive voter fraud"
2 turn public against media that criticize them
"deceitful" "scum"
few press conferences
mass rallies, tweets
3 repeatedly tell big lies
4. blame stresses on immigrants or racial or religious minorities
5 Call critics "enemies"
6 Appoint family members, private security, generals.
7 keep personal finances secret + profit from office.

AN ORGY OF UNNECESSARY CRUELTY

The theme that unites all of Trump's initiatives so far is their unnecessary cruelty.

1) HIS BUDGET COMES DOWN ESPECIALLY HARD ON THE POOR — imposing unprecedented cuts in low-income housing, job training, food assistance, legal services, help to distressed rural communities, nutrition for new mothers and their infants, funds to keep poor families warm, even "Meals on Wheels."

These cuts come at a time when more American families are living in poverty than ever before, including one in five children.

Why is Trump doing this? To pay for the biggest hike in military spending since the 1980s. Yet the United States already spends more on its military than the next seven biggest military budgets put together.

2) HIS PLAN TO REPEAL AND "REPLACE" THE AFFORDABLE CARE ACT will cause 14 million Americans to lose their health insurance in 2018, and 24 million by 2026.

Why is Trump doing this? To bestow $600 billion in tax breaks over the next decade to wealthy Americans. This windfall comes at a time when the rich have accumulated more wealth than at any time in the nation's history.

The plan reduces the federal budget deficit by only $337 billion over the next 10 years — a small fraction of the national debt — in exchange for creating an enormous amount of human hardship.

3) HIS BAN ON SYRIAN REFUGEES and reduction by half in the total number of refugees admitted to the U.S. comes just as the world is experiencing the worst refugee crisis since World War II.

Why is Trump doing this? The ban does little or nothing to protect Americans from terrorism. No terrorist act in the United States has been perpetrated by a Syrian or by anyone from the six nations whose citizens are now banned from traveling here. You have higher odds of being struck by lightning than dying from an immigrant terrorist attack.

4) HIS DRAGNET ROUNDUP OF UNDOCUMENTED IMMIGRANTS IS HELTER-SKELTER — including people who have been productive members of our society for decades and young people who have been here since they were toddlers.

Why is Trump doing this? He has no compelling justification for it. Unemployment is down, crime is down, and we have fewer undocumented workers in the country today than we did five years ago.

Trump is embarking on an orgy of cruelty for absolutely no reason. This is morally repugnant. It violates every ideal this nation has ever cherished.

We have a moral responsibility to stop it. §

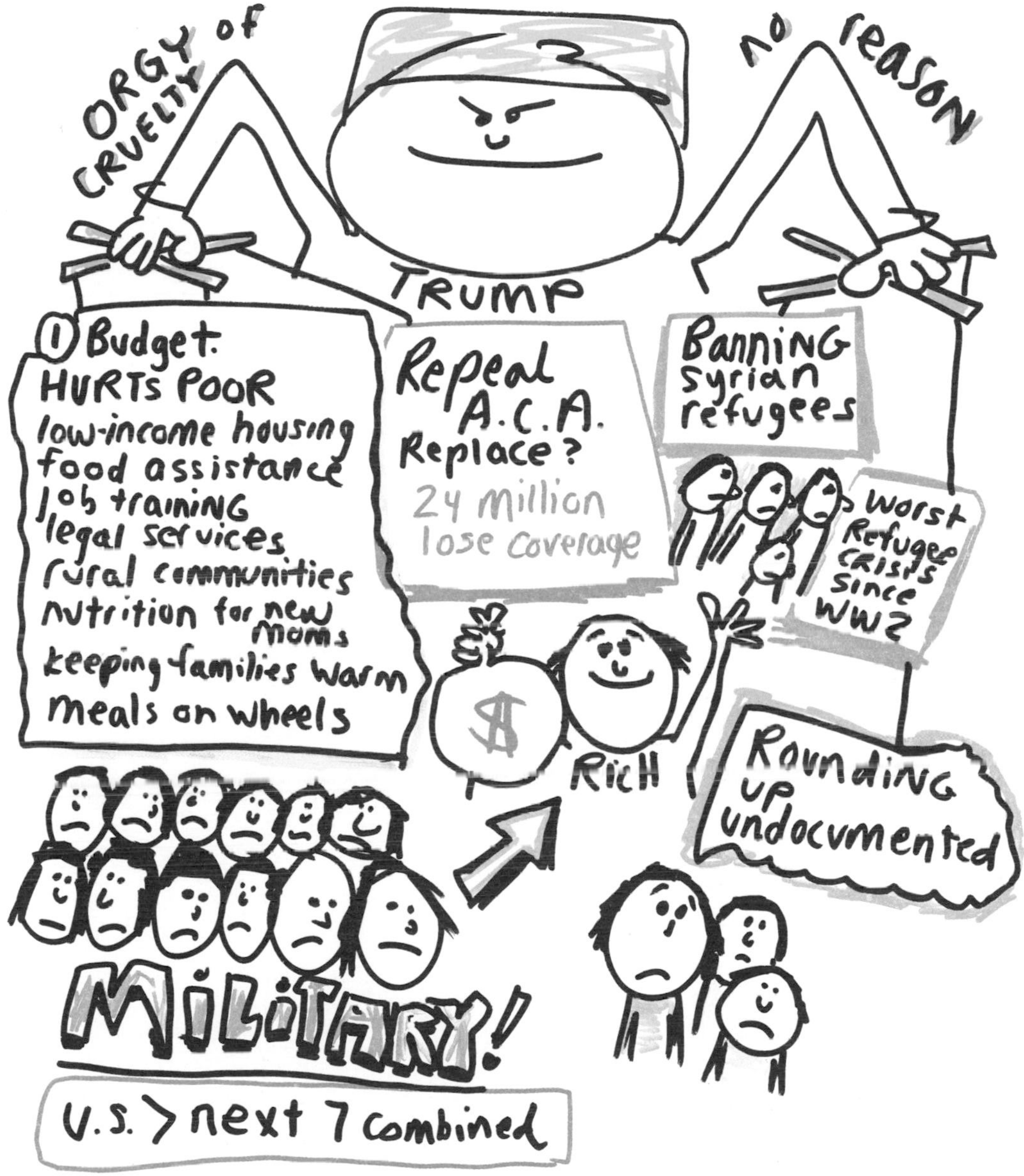
ORGY of CRUELTY
no reason
TRUMP
① Budget.
HURTS POOR
low-income housing
food assistance
job training
legal services
rural communities
nutrition for new moms
keeping families warm
meals on wheels
Repeal A.C.A.
Replace?
24 million lose coverage
Banning Syrian refugees
Worst Refugee Crisis since WW2
RICH
Rounding up undocumented
MILITARY!
U.S. > next 7 combined

TRUMP'S BONKERS BUDGET

Donald Trump ran for president as a man of the people, who was going to fight for those who were left behind. But everything about his federal budget says exactly the opposite.

It's a great deal for big corporations, which have hired armies of lobbyists to promote their interests, and the wealthiest few, like himself, but it leaves almost everyone else a lot worse off.

Here are four important early warning flares:

1) TRUMP'S BUDGET WILL INCREASE MILITARY SPENDING BY 10%, even though U.S. military expenditures already exceed the next seven largest military budgets around the world, combined.

And that's frankly scary for a lot of reasons, from what it signals about his foreign policy priorities to the impact that whopping military spending hike will have on the other parts of the federal budget.

2) TRUMP ACTUALLY PLANS TO CUT CORPORATE TAXES (even though U.S. corporate profits are now higher as a percentage of the economy than they've been since 1947).

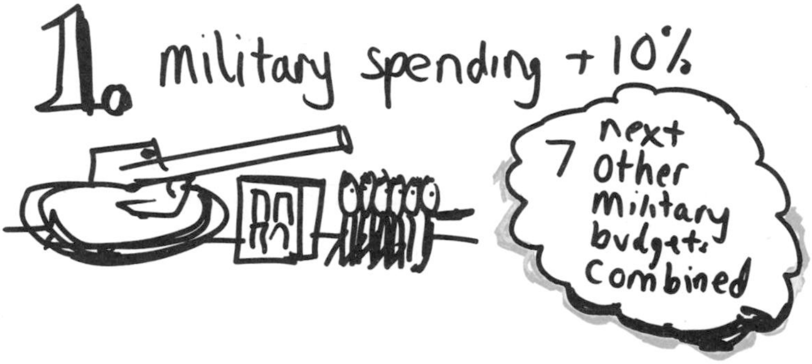
1.
military spending +10%
7 next other military budgets combined

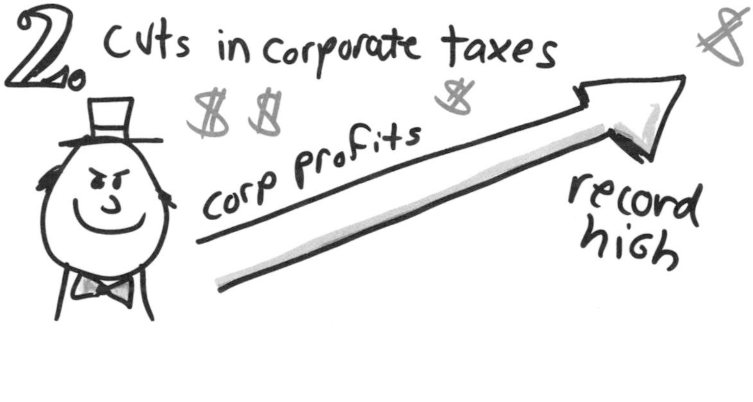
2.
cuts in corporate taxes
corp profits
record high

3) HE'S GOING TO PAY FOR THIS — IN PART — BY CUTTING BILLIONS OF DOLLARS FROM THE ENVIRONMENTAL PROTECTION AGENCY, which would strip the EPA of almost all of its capacity to enforce environmental laws and regulations at a time when climate change threatens the future of the planet. This is precisely the *opposite* of what we ought to be doing.

4) LAST — BUT BY NO MEANS LEAST — HUGE LEAPS IN MILITARY SPENDING COUPLED WITH TAX CUTS WILL MEAN BIG CUTS TO PROGRAMS LIKE FOOD STAMPS AND MEDICAID at a time when the United States has the highest poverty rate among all advanced nations, including more than one in five American children. §

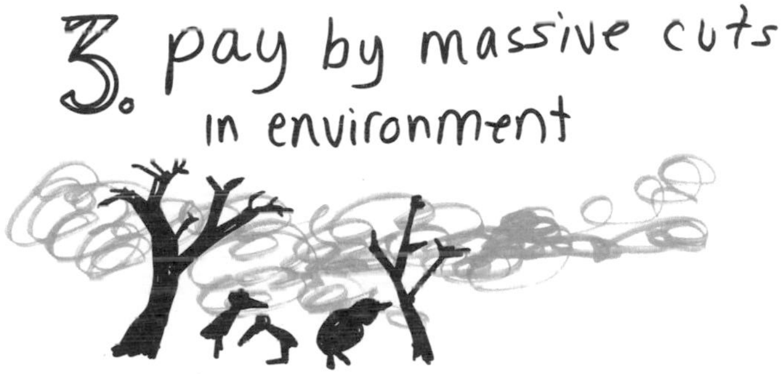
3. pay by massive cuts
in environment

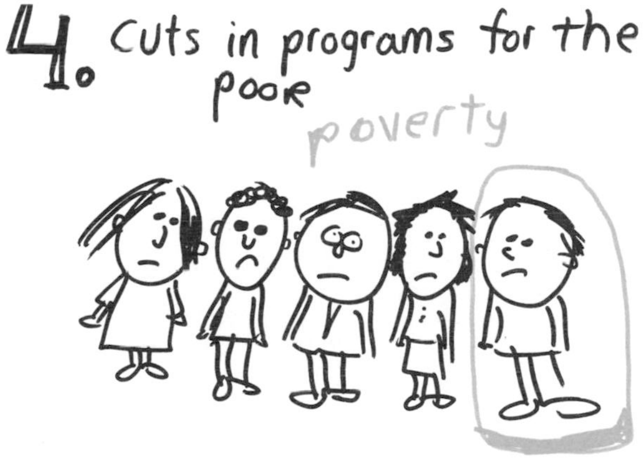
4. cuts in programs for the poor
poverty

TEARING DOWN THE WALL BETWEEN CHURCH AND STATE

Donald Trump may be building a wall along the Mexican border, but he's taking down the wall separating church and state in America.

CONSIDER:

1. TRUMP'S NEW TRAVEL BAN into the United States targets Muslims and exempts Christians.

2. TRUMP'S SECRETARY OF EDUCATION, BETSY DEVOS, has described her work on education reform as a way to "advance God's kingdom." High on her agenda is redirecting taxpayer funds to religious schools.

3. HIS ATTORNEY GENERAL, JEFF SESSIONS, has said the idea of a "wall of separation" between church and state "is not constitutional and is not historical." Sessions has attacked Justice Sonia Sotomayor for having a "postmodern, relativistic, secular mindset. And I believe it is directly contrary to the founding of our republic."

4. TRUMP'S GAG RULE PROHIBITING U.S. FUNDING TO NONGOVERNMENTAL ORGANIZATIONS that offer or even advise family planning and reproductive health options if they include abortion involves a matter of conscience at the heart of personal religious liberty.

5. HIS SECRETARY OF HOUSING AND URBAN DEVELOPMENT, BEN CARSON, has argued that in taking God out of government, "secular progressives have succeeded *de facto* in redefining part of the Constitution."

6. HIS VICE PRESIDENT, MIKE PENCE, has spoken on the House floor criticizing public schools for teaching evolution but not creationism. He said: "Let us demand that educators around America teach evolution not as fact, but as theory. And an interesting theory, to boot."

7. TRUMP'S SECRETARY OF HEALTH AND HUMAN SERVICES, TOM PRICE, has joined Pence in co-sponsoring bills granting full legal personhood to zygotes.

The First Amendment bars any law respecting the establishment of religion or infringing on the free exercise of religion. Trump and his administration are well on the way to violating that fundamental right. §

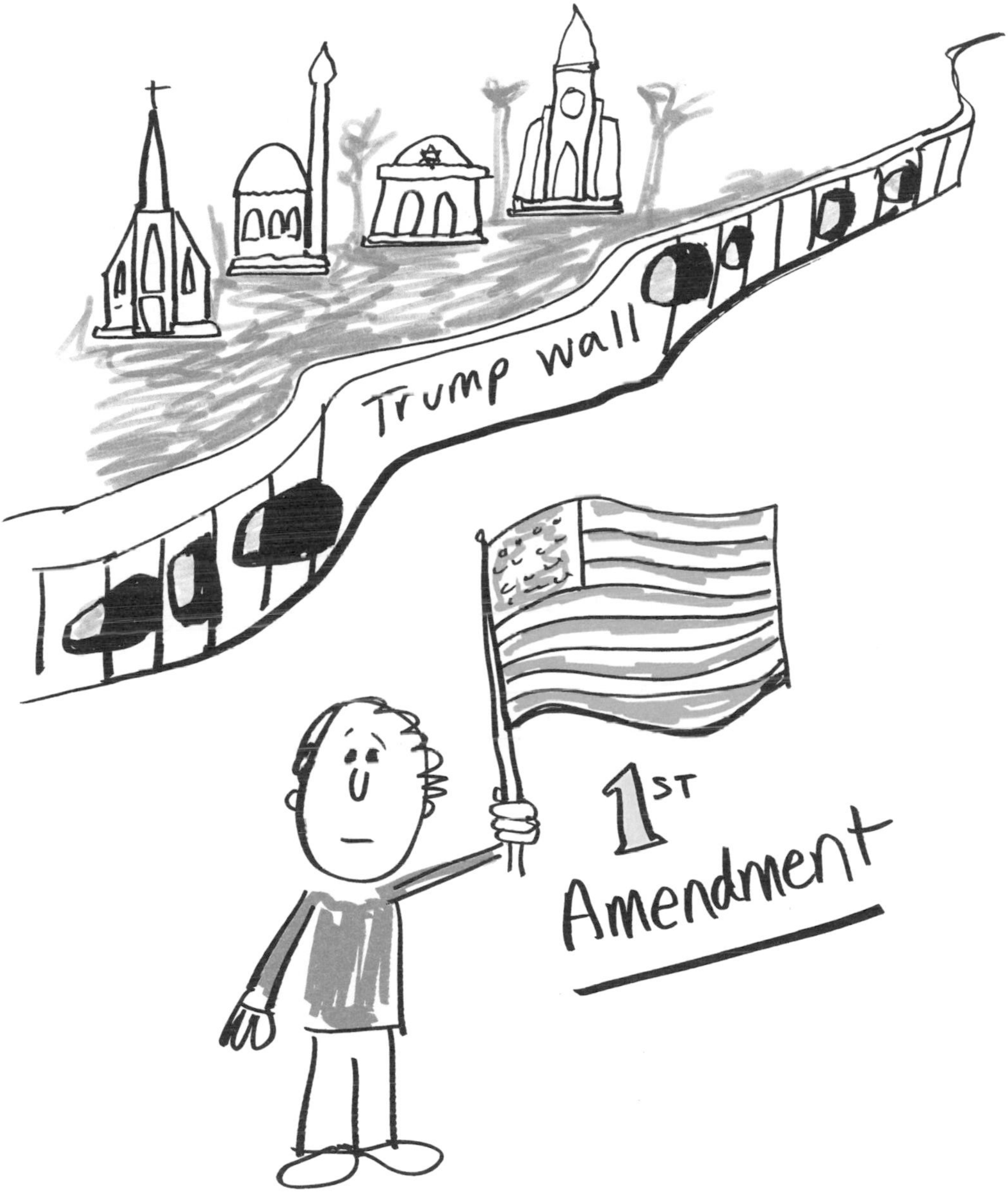
Trump wall
1ST
Amendment

TRUMP'S ATTACK ON THE FREEDOM OF THE PRESS

Historically, tyrants have tried to control the press using four techniques that, worryingly, Donald Trump is already using.

1) BERATE THE MEDIA AND TURN THE PUBLIC AGAINST IT. Trump refers to journalists as "dishonest," "disgusting," and "scum." When Trump lies — claiming, for example, "massive voter fraud" in the election, and that he "won in a landslide" — and the media call him on those lies, Trump claims the media is lying. Even televised satires he labels as "unfunny, one-sided, and pathetic."

2) LIMIT MEDIA ACCESS. Trump has blocked the media from traveling with him — and even from knowing with whom he's meeting. His phone call with Russian President Vladimir Putin — which occurred shortly after the election — was first reported by the Kremlin.

3) THREATEN THE MEDIA. During the campaign, Trump threatened to sue *The New York Times* for libel in response to an article about two women who accused him of touching them inappropriately years ago, and then another that revealed part of his 1995 tax returns. He says he plans to "open up our libel laws so when they write purposely negative and horrible and false articles, we can sue them and win lots of money."

4) BYPASS THE MEDIA AND COMMUNICATE WITH THE PUBLIC DIRECTLY. Trump tweets incessantly, issues videos, and holds large rallies — all of which further enable him to lie directly to the public with impunity.

The word "media" comes from "intermediate" between the powerful and the public. The media hold the powerful accountable by correcting their misstatements, asking them hard questions, and reporting on what they do. Apparently Trump wants to eliminate such intermediaries.

Historically, these four techniques have been used by demagogues to erode the freedom and independence of the press. Donald Trump seems intent on doing exactly that. §

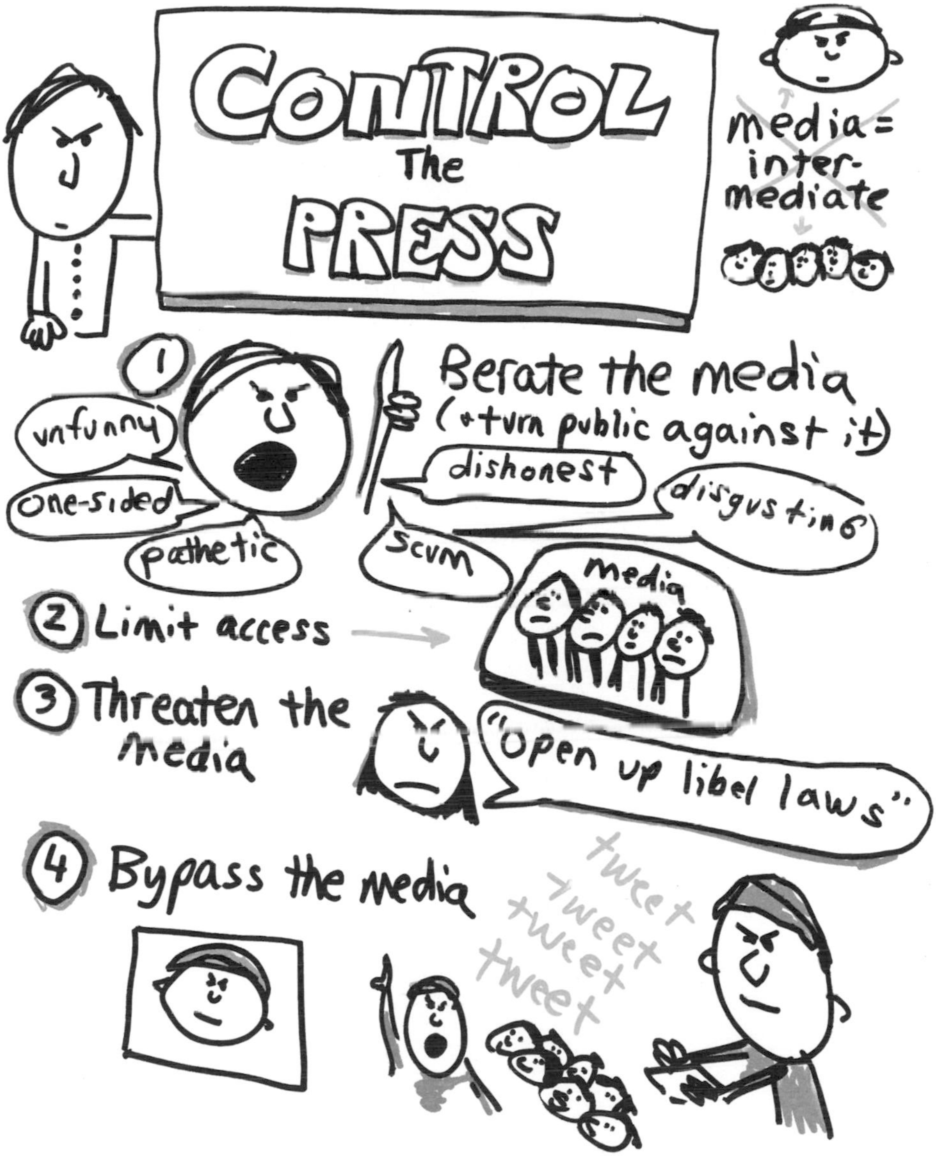
CONTROL The PRESS
media = inter-mediate
① Berate the media (+turn public against it)
unfunny
one-sided
pathetic
dishonest
disgusting
scum
② Limit access
media
③ Threaten the media
"Open up libel laws"
④ Bypass the media
tweet
tweet
tweet
tweet

TRUMP'S TEN STEPS FOR TURNING LIES INTO HALF-TRUTHS

At the beginning of 2017, the *Wall Street Journal's* editor-in-chief insisted that the paper wouldn't label Trump's false statements as "lies." Lying, said the editor, requires a deliberate intention to mislead, which couldn't be proven in Trump's case.

But Donald Trump lies more than any president we've ever had, and he seems to get away with it. Here's his ten-step plan for turning lies into near-truths:

STEP 1) HE LIES.

STEP 2) EXPERTS CONTRADICT HIM, saying his claim is baseless and false. The media report that the claim is false.

STEP 3) TRUMP BLASTS THE EXPERTS and condemns the media for being "dishonest."

STEP 4) TRUMP REPEATS THE LIE in tweets and speeches and asserts that "many people" say he's right.

STEP 5) THE MAINSTREAM MEDIA start to describe the lie as a "disputed fact."

STEP 6) TRUMP REPEATS THE LIE in tweets, interviews, and speeches. His surrogates repeat it on TV and in the right-wing blogosphere.

STEP 7) THE MAINSTREAM MEDIA begin to describe Trump's lie as a "controversy."

STEP 8) POLLS SHOW a growing number of Americans (including most Republicans) believing Trump's lie to be true.

STEP 9) THE MEDIA start describing Trump's lie as "a claim that reflects a partisan divide in America," and is "found to be true by many."

STEP 10) THE PUBLIC IS CONFUSED and disoriented about what the facts are. Trump wins.

Don't let Trump's lies become near-truths. Be vigilant. Know the truth — and spread it.

The media should stop mincing words. Report Trump's lies as lies. §

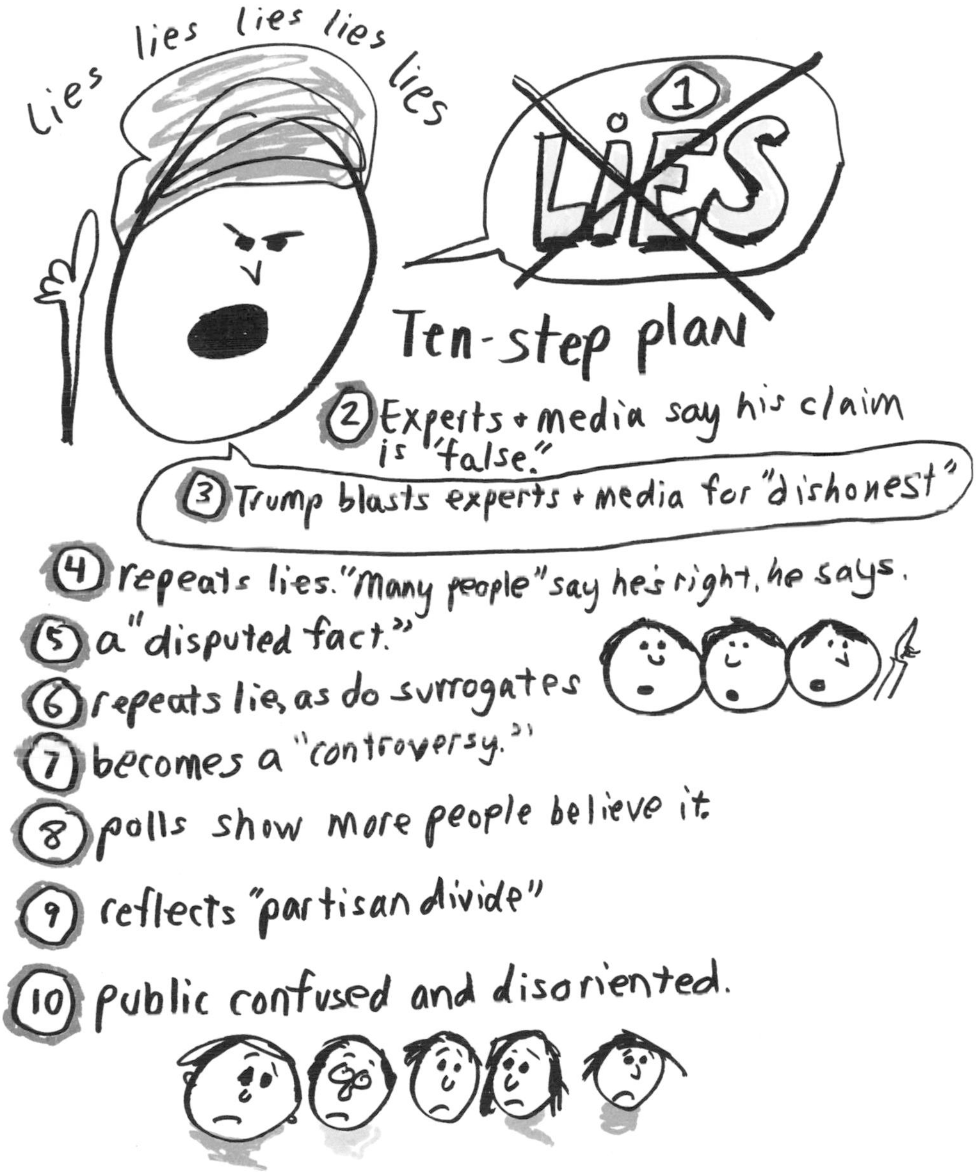
lies lies lies lies lies
LIES
1
Ten-step plan
2 Experts + media say his claim is "false."
3 Trump blasts experts + media for "dishonest"
4 repeats lies. "Many people" say he's right, he says.
5 a "disputed fact."
6 repeats lie, as do surrogates
7 becomes a "controversy."
8 polls show more people believe it.
9 reflects "partisan divide"
10 public confused and disoriented.

TRUMPCARE

The Trumpcare bill passed by the House breaks eight of Trump's promises on healthcare:

1. HE PROMISED "INSURANCE FOR EVERYBODY," but under Trumpcare, millions of Americans will lose coverage.

2. HE PROMISED NOT TO CUT MEDICAID, but Trumpcare slashes Medicaid by $834 billion over 10 years, almost 1/4 of its entire budget. As a result, 14 million people will lose access to healthcare by 2026, according to the nonpartisan Congressional Budget Office.

3. HE PROMISED TO TAKE "CARE OF PRE-EXISTING CONDITIONS." But Trumpcare removes safeguards for people with pre-existing conditions, allowing states to opt out of rules that protect the sick from being charged so much more they wouldn't be able to afford it.

4. HE SAID HE'D "TAKE CARE OF WOMEN WITH WOMEN'S HEALTH ISSUES FAR BETTER THAN HILLARY CLINTON." But Trumpcare cuts funding for Planned Parenthood, could send pregnancy costs skyrocketing, and even opens the door for rape and sexual assault to be considered pre-existing conditions.

5. HE PROMISED PREMIUMS WOULD COME DOWN. But under Trumpcare, premiums are expected to increase over the next two years, especially for people with pre-existing conditions. According to the Center for American Progress, even Americans with relatively mild pre-existing conditions could pay thousands of dollars more.

6. HE PROMISED "YOU'LL HAVE BETTER HEALTHCARE." But Trumpcare allows states to get around rules that require insurers to provide essential health benefits, including maternal care, prescription coverage, and mental healthcare.

7. HE PROMISED "MUCH LOWER DEDUCTIBLES." According to the Congressional Budget Office analysis of the original bill, "deductibles would tend to be higher" under Trump's plan.

8. HE PROMISED HEALTHCARE TO FAMILIES THAT CAN'T AFFORD IT. Not only does Trumpcare dramatically cut Medicaid, it also reduces tax credits for low-income families to get coverage.

Trump's healthcare promises are worse than worthless. If implemented, they will cost most Americans a bundle. They will cost many people their lives. §

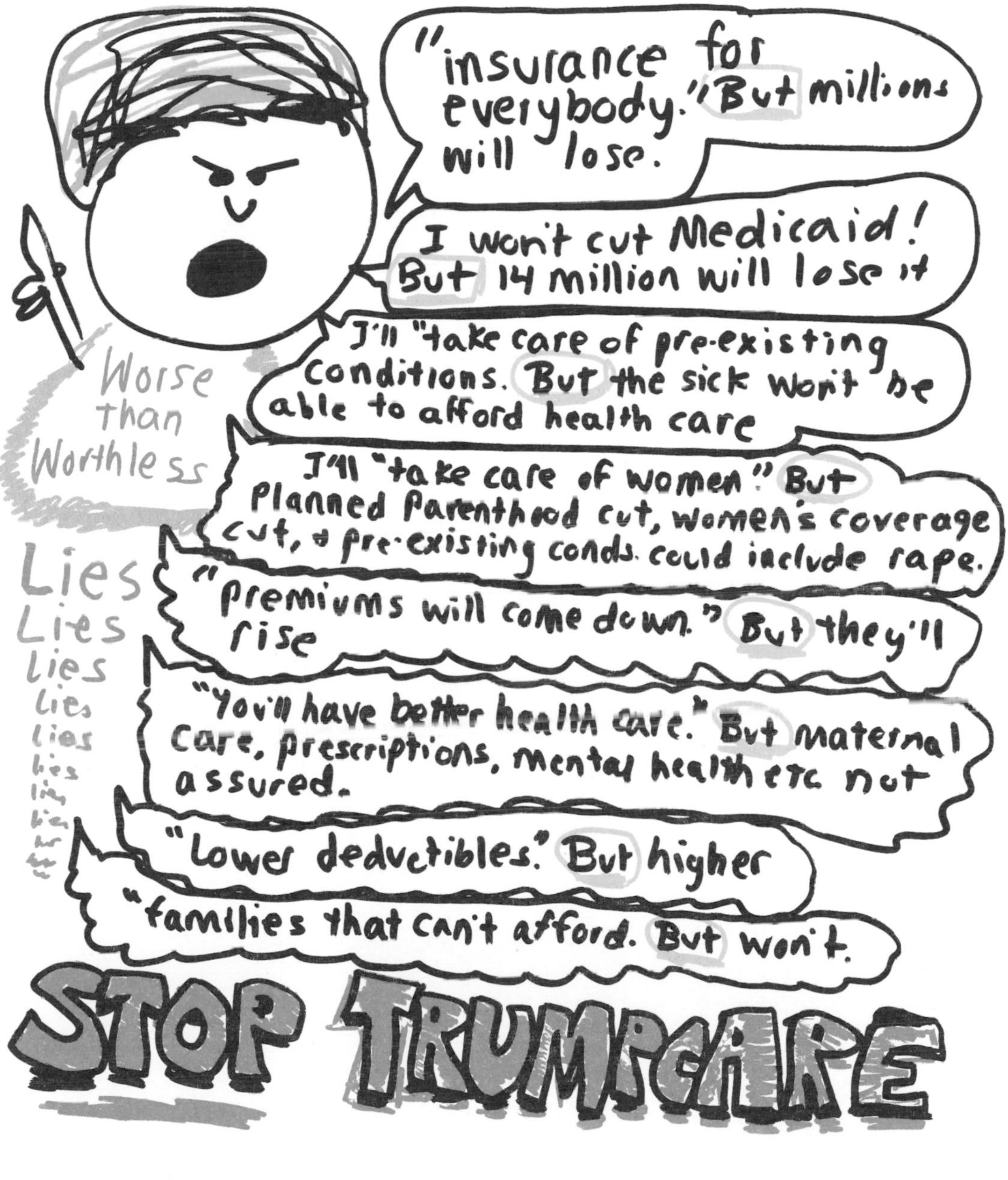
"insurance for everybody." But millions will lose.
I won't cut Medicaid! But 14 million will lose it
I'll "take care of pre-existing conditions. But the sick won't be able to afford health care
I'll "take care of women." But Planned Parenthood cut, women's coverage cut, + pre-existing conds. could include rape.
"premiums will come down." But they'll rise
"You'll have better health care." But maternal care, prescriptions, mental health etc not assured.
"Lower deductibles." But higher
"families that can't afford. But won't.
Worse than Worthless
Lies Lies lies
STOP TRUMPCARE

TRUMP'S INFRASTRUCTURE SCAM

Our country is in dire need of massive investments in infrastructure, but what Donald Trump is proposing is nothing more than a huge tax giveaway for the rich.

1) IT'S A GIANT PUBLIC SUBSIDY TO DEVELOPERS AND INVESTORS. Rather than taxing the wealthy and then using the money to fix our dangerously outdated roads, bridges, airports, and water systems, Trump wants to give rich developers and Wall Street investors tax credits to encourage them to do it. That means that for every dollar they put into a project, they'd actually pay only 18 cents, and we would contribute the other 82 cents through our tax dollars.

2) WE'D BE TURNING OVER PUBLIC ROADS AND BRIDGES TO PRIVATE CORPORATIONS THAT WILL CHARGE US EXPENSIVE TOLLS AND EARN BIG PROFITS. Those tolls will be set high in order to satisfy the profit margins demanded by elite Wall Street investors. So, essentially, we pay twice: once when we subsidize the developers and investors with our tax dollars, and then again when we pay the tolls and user fees that also go into their pockets.

3) WE GET THE WRONG KIND OF INFRASTRUCTURE. Projects that will be most attractive to Wall Street investors are those whose tolls and fees bring in the biggest bucks — giant mega-projects like major new throughways and new bridges. Not the thousands of smaller bridges, airports, pipes, and water treatment facilities most in need of repair. Not the needs of rural communities and smaller cities and towns too small to generate the tolls and other user fees that equity investors want. Not clean energy.

To really make America great again, we need more and better infrastructure for the public — not for big developers and investors. And the only way we get that is if corporations and the wealthy pay their fair share of taxes. §

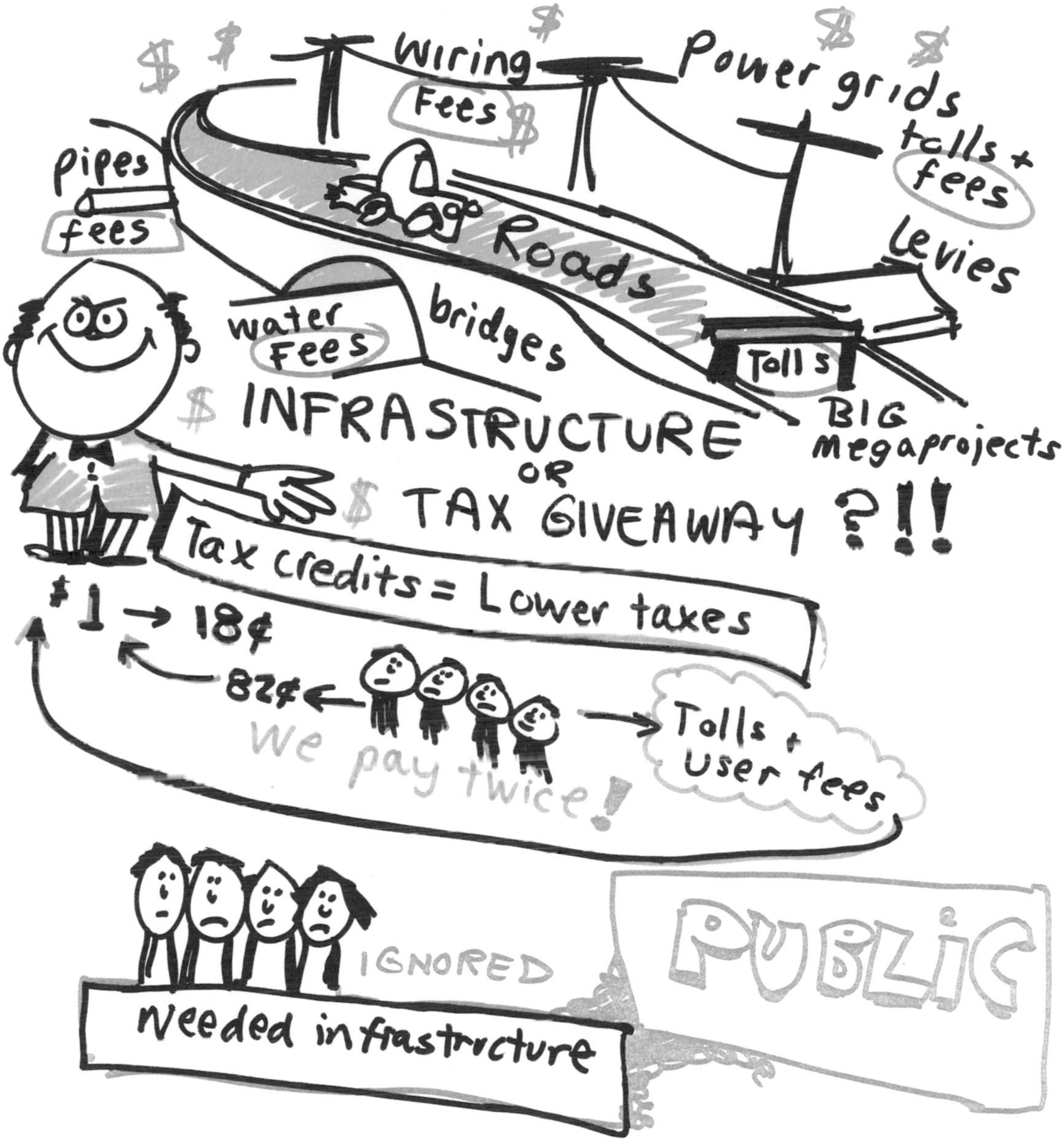
Wiring
Fees
Power grids
tolls + fees
pipes
fees
Roads
levies
water Fees
bridges
Tolls
INFRASTRUCTURE
OR
TAX GIVEAWAY ?!!
BIG Megaprojects
Tax credits = Lower taxes
$1 → 18¢
82¢
Tolls + User fees
We pay twice!
IGNORED
PUBLIC
Needed infrastructure

TRUMP'S BIG BET ON COAL

When Donald Trump was running for president, he talked a lot about putting people back to work.

One of the industries he focused on most was the coal industry. He even put on a hard hat and waved around a pickaxe to show how much he loved coal.

But there simply aren't very many coal jobs to be had anymore in the U.S. That's not because of anything Obama did. Coal jobs are decreasing because demand for coal is decreasing, and because machines now do much of the work.

In 1985, the American coal industry employed a little over 178,000 miners. By 2016, it employed just 56,000.

By contrast, in 2016, wind and solar energy provided more than six times the number of jobs as coal. The trend is toward even more jobs in wind and solar, regardless of what Trump does.

Solar energy is exploding worldwide — an almost sixfold increase in just the last five years. But America ranks fifth in the production of solar energy — behind China, Germany, Japan, and Italy.

If we really want to lead — if we really want to join the new energy economy — we have to go with the energy of the future, not the energy of the past.

The other option — the one Donald Trump proposes — leaves us following, not leading. §

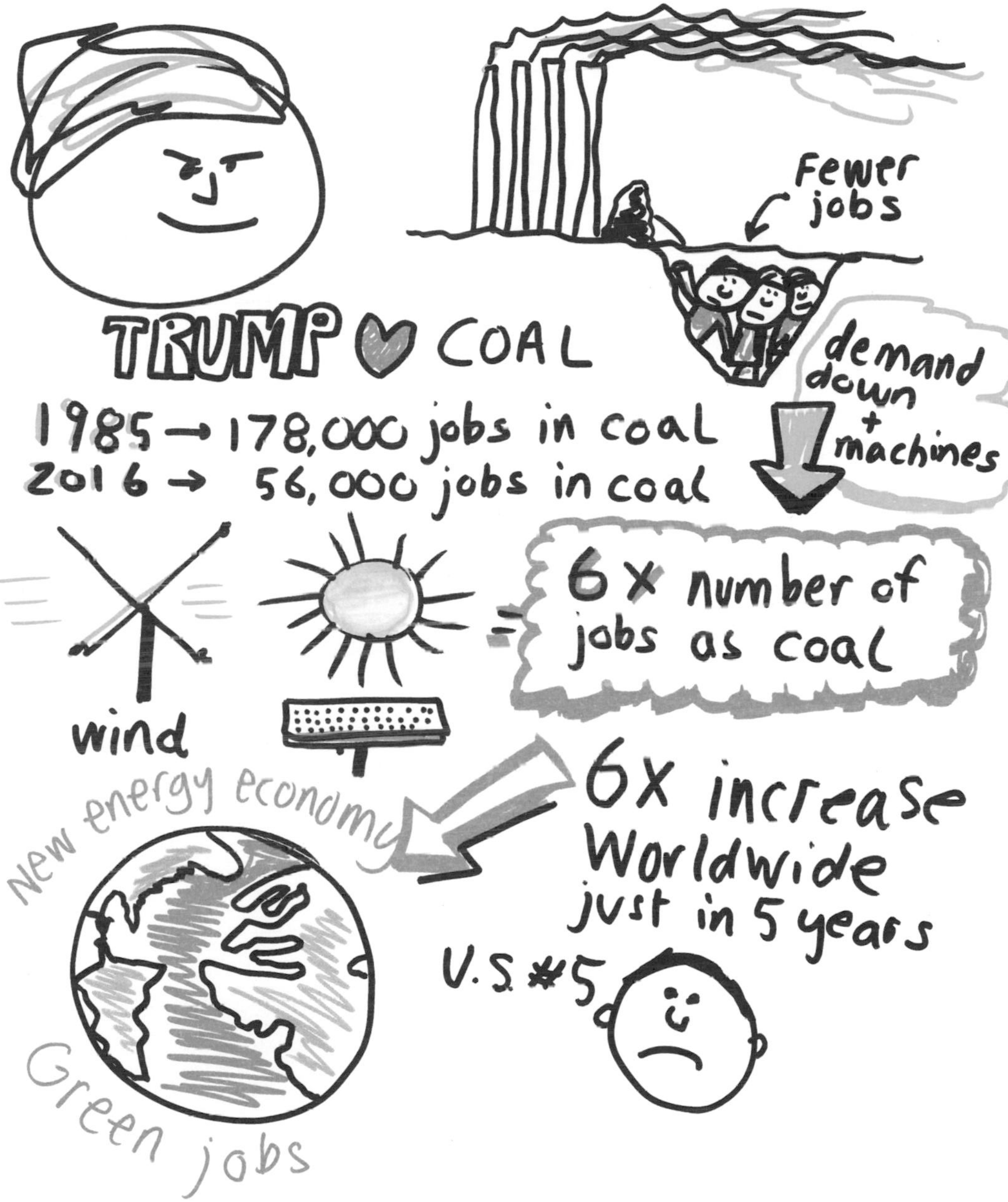
Fewer jobs
TRUMP COAL
demand down + machines
1985 → 178,000 jobs in coal
2016 → 56,000 jobs in coal
6 x number of jobs as coal
wind
New energy economy
6X increase Worldwide just in 5 years
U.S. #5
Green jobs

THE WALL

The "big idea" that Trump keeps peddling is to build a wall between the United States and Mexico. That's as dumb an idea as it is racist and xenophobic, and here's why:

1) THE COST OF TRUMP'S FENCE would be a whopping $25 billion. That's the best estimate I've seen by a *Washington Post* fact checker. When Trump discussed the cost last February he put it at $8 billion, then a few weeks later he upped the cost to $10 to $12 billion. So far, he doesn't have anywhere near the budget to complete the wall.

2) TRUMP SAYS WE DON'T NEED TO WORRY about the actual cost because Mexico will pay. But there's no way Mexico will pay for it. On January 11, 2017, Mexican President Enrique Peña Nieto assured Mexicans they would not be footing the bill. That means American taxpayers will have to pay for this massive undertaking that's sure to fail.

3) THERE'S NO REASON FOR THE WALL ANYWAY because undocumented migration from Mexico has sharply declined. The Department of Homeland Security's estimates that the total undocumented population peaked at 12 million in 2008, and has fallen since then. According to the Pew Research Center, the overall flow of Mexican immigrants between the two countries is at its smallest since the 1990s. The number of apprehensions at the border is at its lowest since 1973.

4) THERE'S LITTLE OR NO EVIDENCE UNDOCUMENTED IMMIGRANTS TAKE JOBS AWAY from Americans, anyway.

A new analysis of U.S. Census data finds that unauthorized immigrants take very different jobs than American citizens. In fact, the United States already allows a significant amount of legal immigration from Mexico under the guest worker program — 1.6 million entries by legal immigrants and 3.9 million by temporary workers from Mexico over the last 10 years.

Of course, Trump lives in a fact-free universe designed merely to enhance his power and fuel his demagoguery. But you don't have to, and nor does anyone else. §

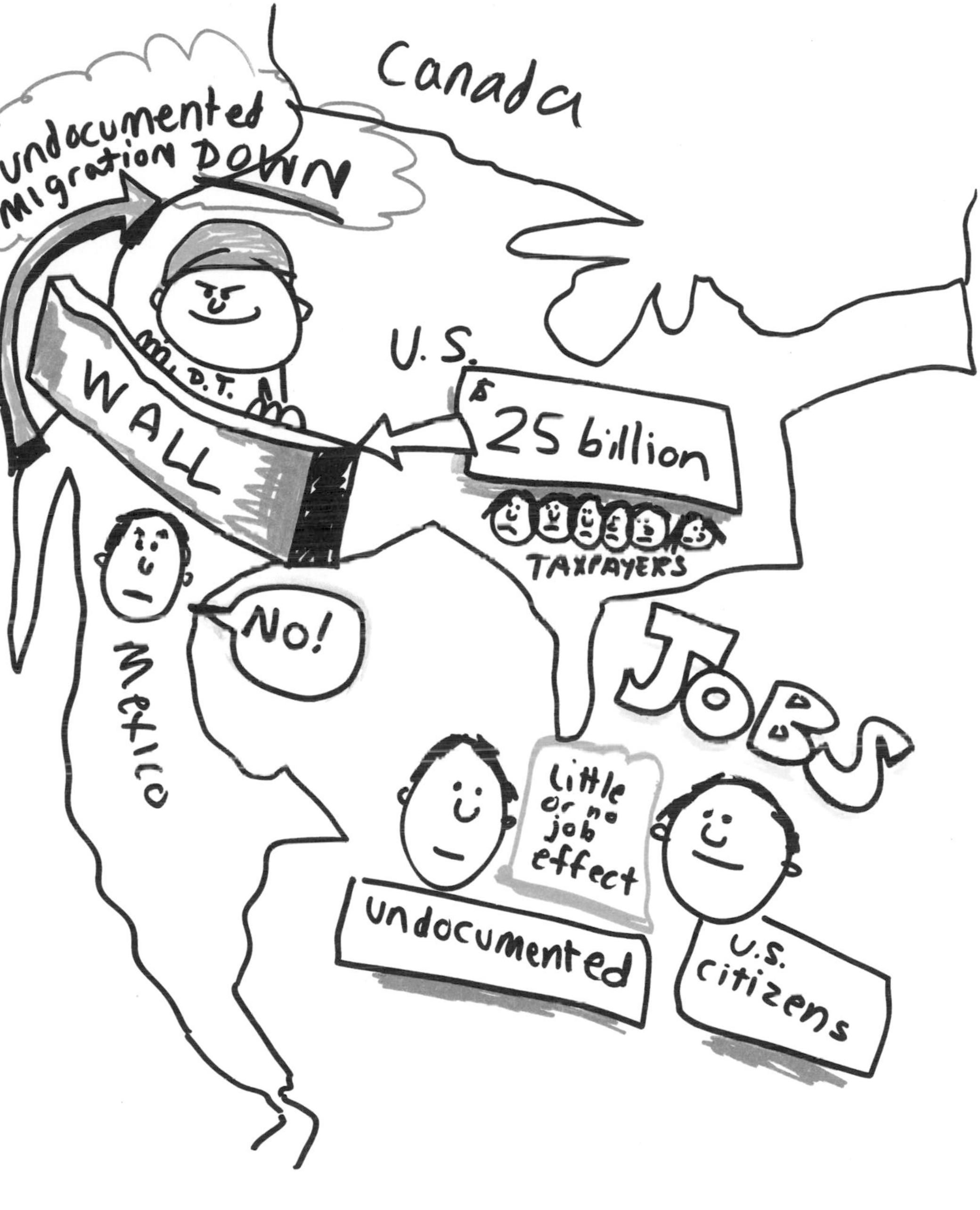
Canada
undocumented migration DOWN
D.T.
WALL
U.S.
$25 billion
TAXPAYERS
No!
Mexico
JOBS
little or no job effect
undocumented
U.S. citizens

TRUMP'S CORPORATE TAX CUTS

Donald Trump wants to cut the corporate income tax rate from 35% to 15%, in order to "make the United States more competitive."

This is nonsensical, for seven reasons:

1) THE GOVERNMENT ACCOUNTABILITY OFFICE DETERMINED THAT PROFITABLE U.S. CORPORATIONS PAID ONLY A 14% EFFECTIVE TAX RATE, on average, between 2008 and 2012. That's less than a lot of middle-class families pay. (And less than half the official 35% corporate tax rate.) What's more, some giant corporations pay little (if any) U.S. taxes because of loopholes or because they shift their profits offshore to tax havens.

2) TRUMP'S CORPORATE TAX CUT WILL BUST THE FEDERAL BUDGET. The nonpartisan Tax Policy Center projects it will reduce federal revenue by $2.4 trillion over 10 years. This will either require huge cuts in services for all of us or additional taxes paid by us to pick up the corporate tab.

3) THIS IS SUPPLY-SIDE, TRICKLE-DOWN NONSENSE: the White House says the tax cuts will create a jump in economic growth that will generate enough new revenue to wipe out any increase in the budget deficit. Ronald Reagan and George W. Bush both cut taxes mostly for the rich, and both ended their presidencies with huge budget deficits.

4) TRUMP'S PLAN WILL CREATE A NEW SPECIAL LOOPHOLE that allows hedge fund managers, big law firms, and real estate moguls like Donald Trump to slash the pass-through tax rate they pay on their business income — dropping it from 40% to 15%. Fifteen percent is what a middle-class person pays. Do you think people like

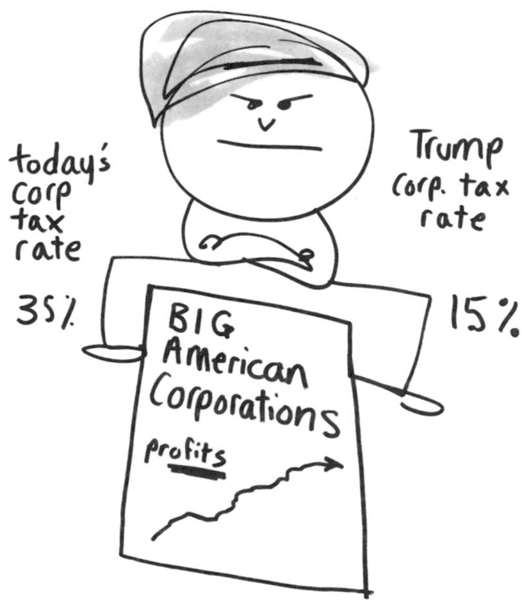
today's corp tax rate
35%
Trump corp. tax rate
15%
BIG American Corporations
profits

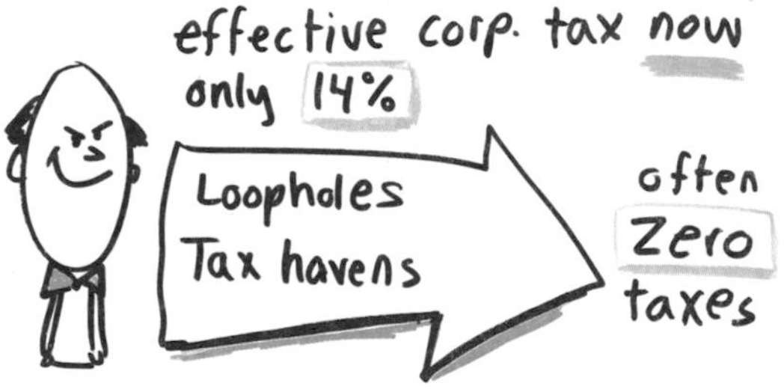
effective corp. tax now only 14%
Loopholes
Tax havens
often zero taxes

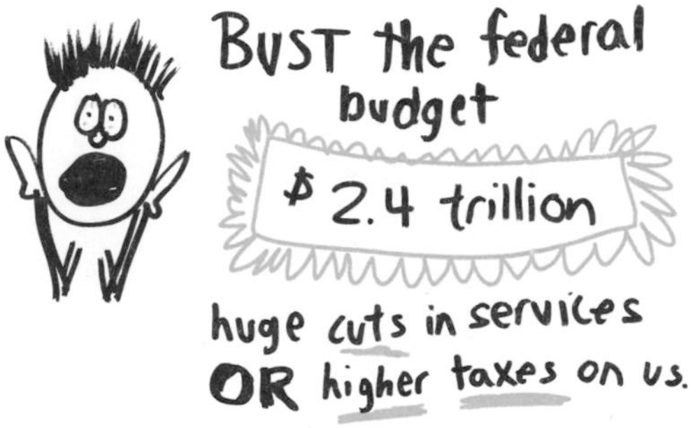
BUST the federal budget
$2.4 trillion
huge cuts in services
OR higher taxes on us.

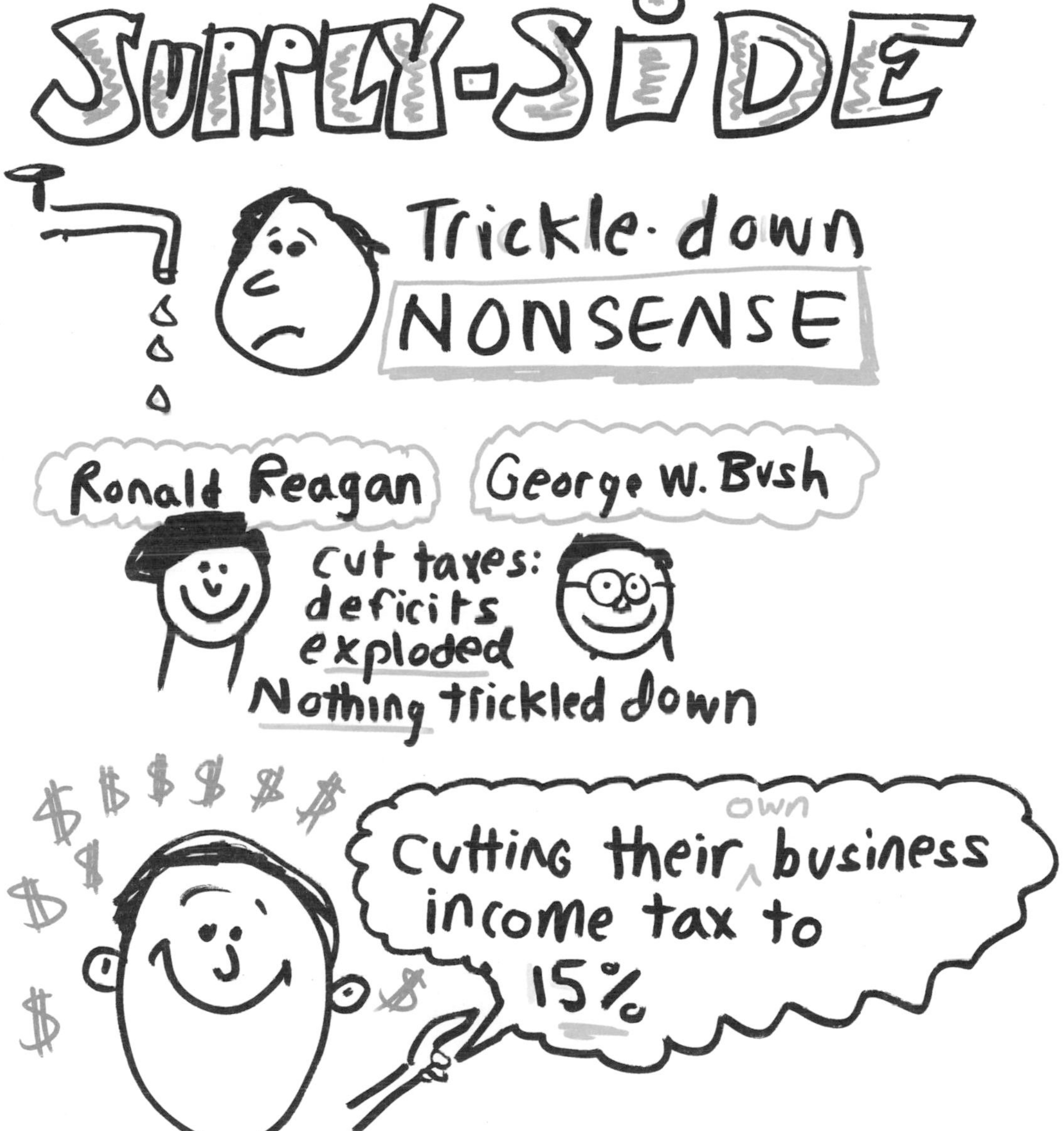
SUPPLY-SIDE
Trickle-down
NONSENSE
Ronald Reagan
George W. Bush
cut taxes:
deficits
exploded
Nothing trickled down
Cutting their own business
income tax to
15%

International race

United States

Italy

Germany

U.K.

France

Brazil

bottom

Tax Havens

profits ↗ record highs

taxes ↘ record lows

BIG Corporations

Trump should pay the same tax rate as someone making $60,000 a year?

5) TRUMP'S PLAN CREATES AN INTERNATIONAL RACE TO THE BOTTOM on corporate tax rates that the U.S. can't win. One of its supposed attractions is that it makes U.S. corporate taxes more "competitive" internationally. But we can't match the rates in tax havens, which are often *zero*. And other countries will just lower their taxes in response. That's what happened after 1986, the last time the U.S. cut corporate tax rates.

6) AMERICAN CORPORATIONS DON'T NEED A TAX CUT. They're already hugely competitive as measured by their profits — which are near record highs — while the share of taxes they pay is at record lows. Corporations should be doing more to pay their fair share, not getting a giant tax cut!

7) THE CLAIM THAT CORPORATIONS WILL USE THE EXTRA PROFITS THEY GET FROM THE TAX CUT TO INVEST IN MORE CAPACITY AND JOBS IS RUBBISH. Corporations are now using a large portion of their profits to pay their CEOs hefty pay packages and to buy other companies in order to raise their stock prices. There's no reason to suppose they'll do any different with even more profits.

Don't fall for Trump's corporate tax plan. It will be a huge windfall for corporations and billionaires — like many of Trump's own cabinet members, family members, and likely even Trump himself — though because he won't release his taxes, we can't tell how much he'll enrich himself from his own tax plan.

But we do know who will lose out: the rest of us. §

what will they do with their tax cut?

- Executive pay
- Buying other companies
- Buying back their stock

not more jobs, better wages

Tax plan a huge windfall

Cabinet member $
Family member $
Trump ⟶ $ Release your taxes!
Other wealthy

Losers ⟶

TRUMP AND BIG BANKS WANT TO REPEAL DODD-FRANK

Donald Trump has ordered a rollback of regulations over Wall Street, including the Dodd-Frank Act, passed in 2010 to prevent another too-big-to-fail banking crisis.

Perhaps he thinks that we've forgotten what happened when Wall Street turned the economy into a giant casino, and then, when its bets went sour in 2008, needed a taxpayer-funded bailout.

Maybe he thinks Americans have forgotten about losing their jobs, homes, and savings in the fallout.

Many people who voted for Trump got shafted. I hope they haven't forgotten that while they suffered, not a single bank executive went to jail. This shouldn't be partisan. Trump supporters need to join with Democrats and progressives in holding Trump accountable.

The biggest banks are far bigger today than they were in 2008. Then, the five largest had 25% of U.S. banking assets. Today they have 44%. If they were too big to fail then, they're too big, period, now.

Getting rid of Dodd-Frank triples the odds of another financial crisis.

Meanwhile, Trump has brought more banksters into his administration than any in any previous administration. Mostly from Goldman Sachs.

The head of Trump's economic council is Gary Cohn who was president of Goldman Sachs. Other Goldman alumni include Trump's right-hand man, Steve Bannon, Trump's Secretary of the Treasury, Steve Mnuchin, Trump's pick for the Securities and Exchange Commission, Jay Clayton, and another White House advisor, Dina Powell.

Now remember, a decade ago, Goldman Sachs defrauded investors and ripped off its customers, and it's paid nearly $9 billion to the government in fines. Many of Trump's banksters were there.

Don't let Trump and the Republicans endanger our economy again. Let's not make the same mistake twice. §

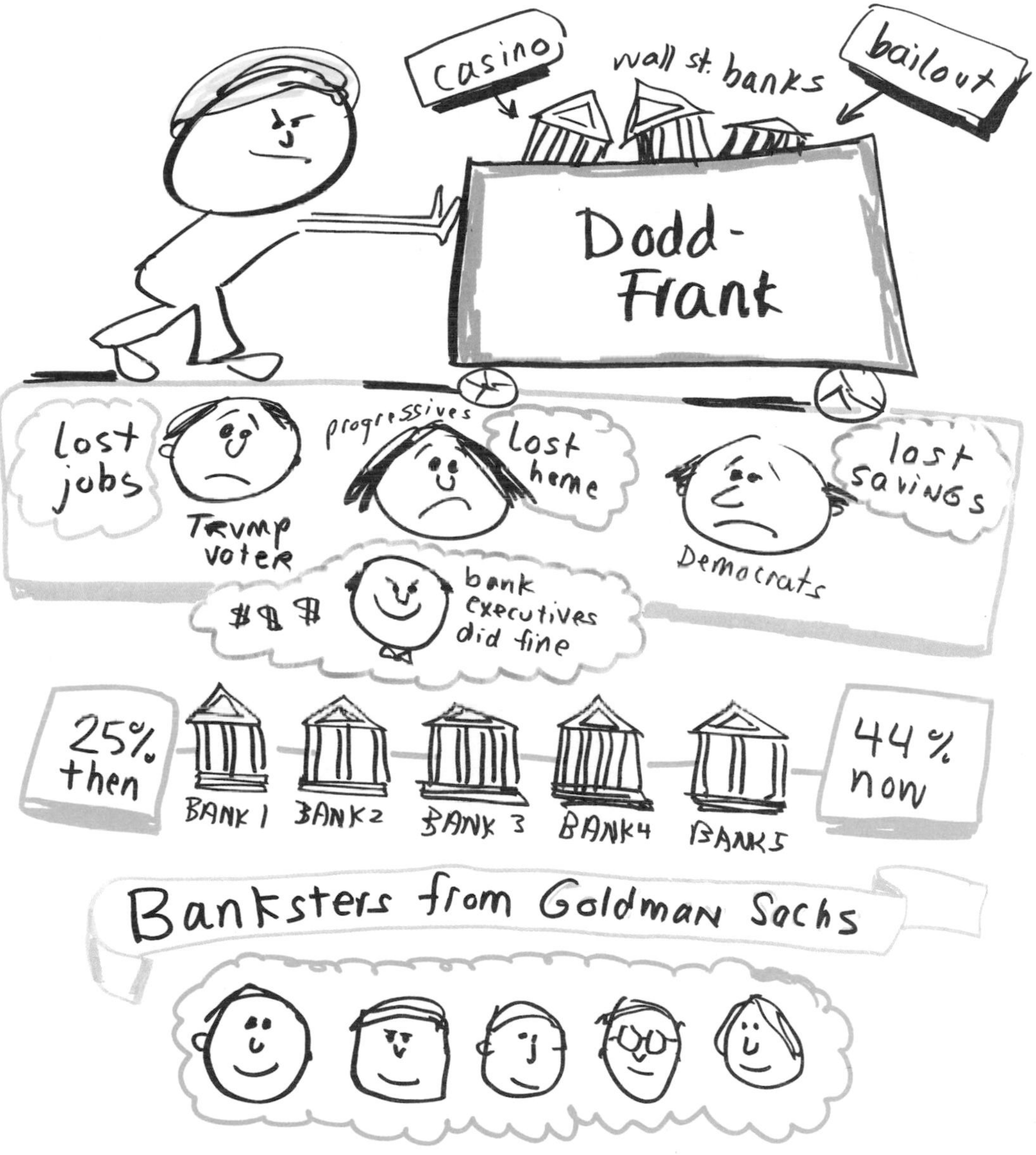
casino
wall st. banks
bailout
Dodd-Frank
lost jobs
Trump voter
progressives
lost home
lost savings
Democrats
$$$
bank executives did fine
25% then
BANK 1
BANK 2
BANK 3
BANK 4
BANK 5
44% now
Banksters from Goldman Sachs

FOUR REASONS WHY TRUMP'S PLAN TO STRIP THE IRS IS INCREDIBLY DUMB

Donald Trump has proposed a 14.1% cut in the budget of the Internal Revenue Service for 2018. This is incredibly dumb, for four reasons:

1) IT WON'T SAVE MONEY. To the contrary, this move worsens the budget deficit. That's because every dollar spent by the IRS to collect taxes generates $4 in unpaid taxes.

2) IT WORSENS THE FEDERAL BUDGET DEFICIT. The current estimate of unpaid taxes per year is almost as large as the federal government's annual budget deficit.

3) IT WIDENS INEQUALITY. Since most IRS audits are of high-income people, the real beneficiaries of Trump's move will be the wealthy, more of whom will then be able to skirt their duty to pay taxes.

4) THE IRS IS ALREADY UNDERSTAFFED. The number of individual tax return audits fell last year to its lowest level since 2004, and enforcement levels were already down by nearly 30% from 2010.

Donald Trump hates the IRS and has spent years battling it. There is reason to think he doesn't even want to pay his own taxes. But this is no reason to explode the federal budget deficit and give another windfall to the rich. §

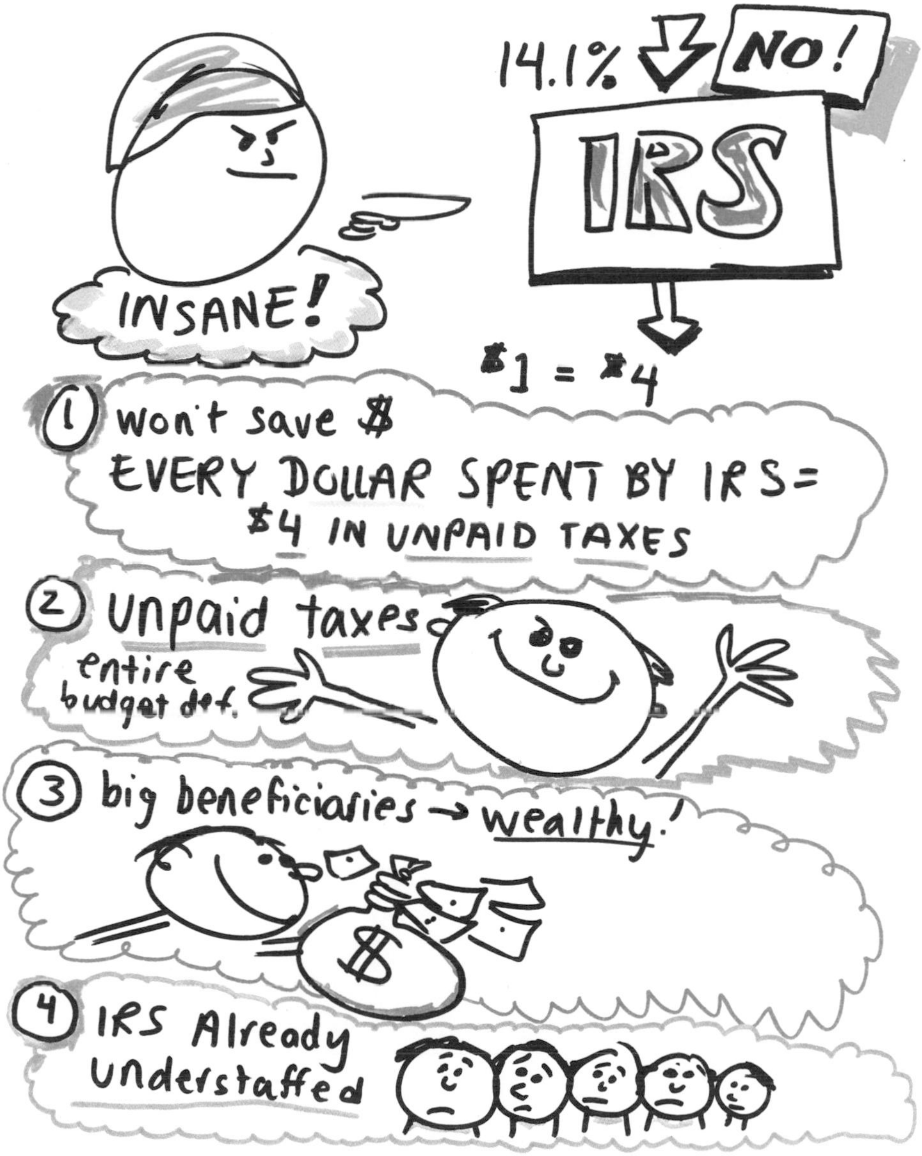
14.1%
NO!
IRS
INSANE!
$1 = $4
1 won't save $
EVERY DOLLAR SPENT BY IRS =
$4 IN UNPAID TAXES
2 unpaid taxes
entire budget def.
3 big beneficiaries → wealthy!
$
4 IRS Already understaffed

THE FOUR DANGEROUS SYNDROMES OF COPING WITH TRUMP

With Donald Trump as president, some of you may be tempted to succumb to one of the following four syndromes. Please don't.

1) **NORMALIZER SYNDROME.** You want to believe Trump is just another president — more conservative than most, but one who will make rational decisions. You're under a grave delusion. Trump and his ultra-conservative cabinet pose a clear and present danger to America and to the world.

2) **OUTRAGE NUMBNESS SYNDROME.** You are no longer outraged by what Trump says or does because you've gone numb. You can't conceive that someone like this is our president so you've shut down emotionally. Maybe you've even stopped reading the news. Please get back in touch and re-engage with what's happening.

3) **CYNICAL SYNDROME.** You've become so cynical about the whole system — the Democrats who gave up on the working class, the Republicans who suppressed votes around the country, the media that gave Trump free airtime, the establishment that rigged the system — that you say the hell with it. Let Trump do his worst. Well, you need to wake up. It can get a lot worse.

4) **HELPLESS SYNDROME.** You aren't in denial. You know that nothing about this is normal, and you desperately want to do something to prevent what's about to occur. But you don't know what to do. You feel utterly helpless, powerless, and immobilized.

Instead of falling prey to one of these syndromes, I urge you to take action — demonstrate, make a ruckus, join with others, demand that your member of Congress also resists. Commit yourself to changing American politics.

Fighting Trump will empower you. And with that power, you will not only minimize the damage, but also get this nation and the world back on the course it must be on. §

Normalizer
outrage numbness
cynical
helpless
Action!
change!
Politics!
Demon-strate
ruckus
join with others
M.O.C.

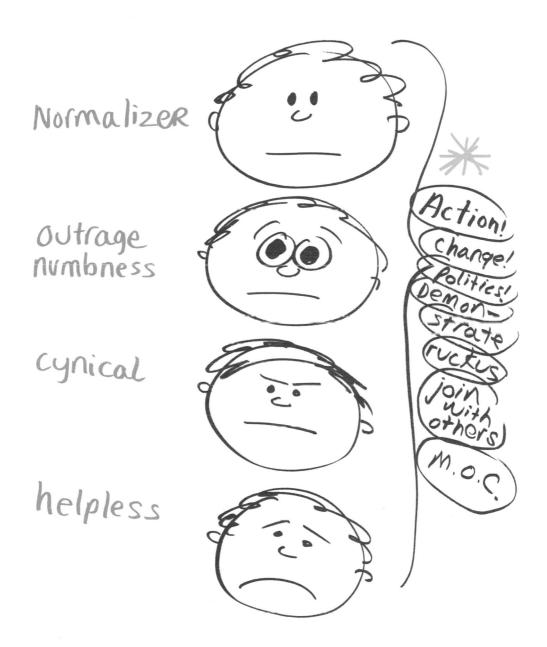

IMPEACHMENT: A HOW-TO EXPLAINER

No president in American history has been convicted on articles of impeachment. Only two presidents so far have been impeached. The first was Andrew Johnson, in 1868. The Senate fell one vote short of convicting him. The next was Bill Clinton, 131 years later, in 1999. Fifty senators voted to convict Clinton, 17 votes short of what was required.

Richard Nixon resigned his office before the House of Representatives had even voted on articles of impeachment. Then Gerald Ford, Nixon's successor, who had been his vice president, gave Nixon a full and unconditional pardon.

The impeachment process revolves around Article I, Sections 2 and 3 of the Constitution, and the rules in the House and the Senate that implement those provisions. Here's how it works.

1) IT STARTS IN THE HOUSE JUDICIARY COMMITTEE, when a majority of the members of the committee vote in favor of what's called an "inquiry of impeachment" resolution.

2) THAT RESOLUTION GOES TO THE FULL HOUSE OF REPRESENTATIVES where a majority has to a) vote in favor and b) vote to authorize and fund a full investigation by the Judiciary Committee into whether sufficient grounds exist for impeachment.

3) THE HOUSE JUDICIARY COMMITTEE INVESTIGATES. That investigation does not have to start from scratch. It can rely on data and conclusions of other investigations undertaken by, say, the FBI.

4) A MAJORITY OF THE JUDICIARY COMMITTEE MEMBERS DECIDES there are sufficient grounds for impeachment, and the Committee issues a "Resolution of Impeachment," setting forth specific allegations of misconduct in one or more articles of impeachment.

5) THE FULL HOUSE THEN CONSIDERS THAT RESOLUTION and votes in favor of it — as a whole or on each article separately. The full House is not bound by the Committee's work. The House may vote to impeach even if the Committee doesn't recommend impeachment.

6) THE MATTER THEN GOES TO THE SENATE FOR A TRIAL. The House's Resolution of Impeachment becomes, in effect, the charges in that trial.

7) THE SENATE ISSUES A SUMMONS TO THE PRESIDENT, who is now effectively the defendant — informing him of the charges and the date by which he has to answer them. If the president chooses not to answer or appear, it's as if he entered a "not guilty" plea.

8) TRIAL IN THE SENATE BEGINS. In that trial, those who are representing the House (the prosecution) and the counsel for the president (the defendant), make opening arguments. They then introduce evidence and put on witnesses, as in any trial. Witnesses are subject to examination and cross-examination. The trial is presided over by the Chief Justice of the Supreme Court — who has the authority to rule on evidentiary questions or may put such questions to a vote of the Senate. The House managers and counsel for the president then make closing arguments.

9) THE SENATE MEETS IN CLOSED SESSION TO DELIBERATE.

10) THE SENATE RETURNS IN OPEN SESSION TO VOTE on whether to convict the president on the articles of impeachment. Conviction requires a two-thirds vote by Senators present. Conviction on one or more articles of impeachment results in removal of the president from office. Such a conviction also disqualifies the now former president from holding any other public office. But it does not bar additional legal proceedings against that former president.

So there you have it — the 10 steps that must all take place to impeach the president. It may come in handy. §

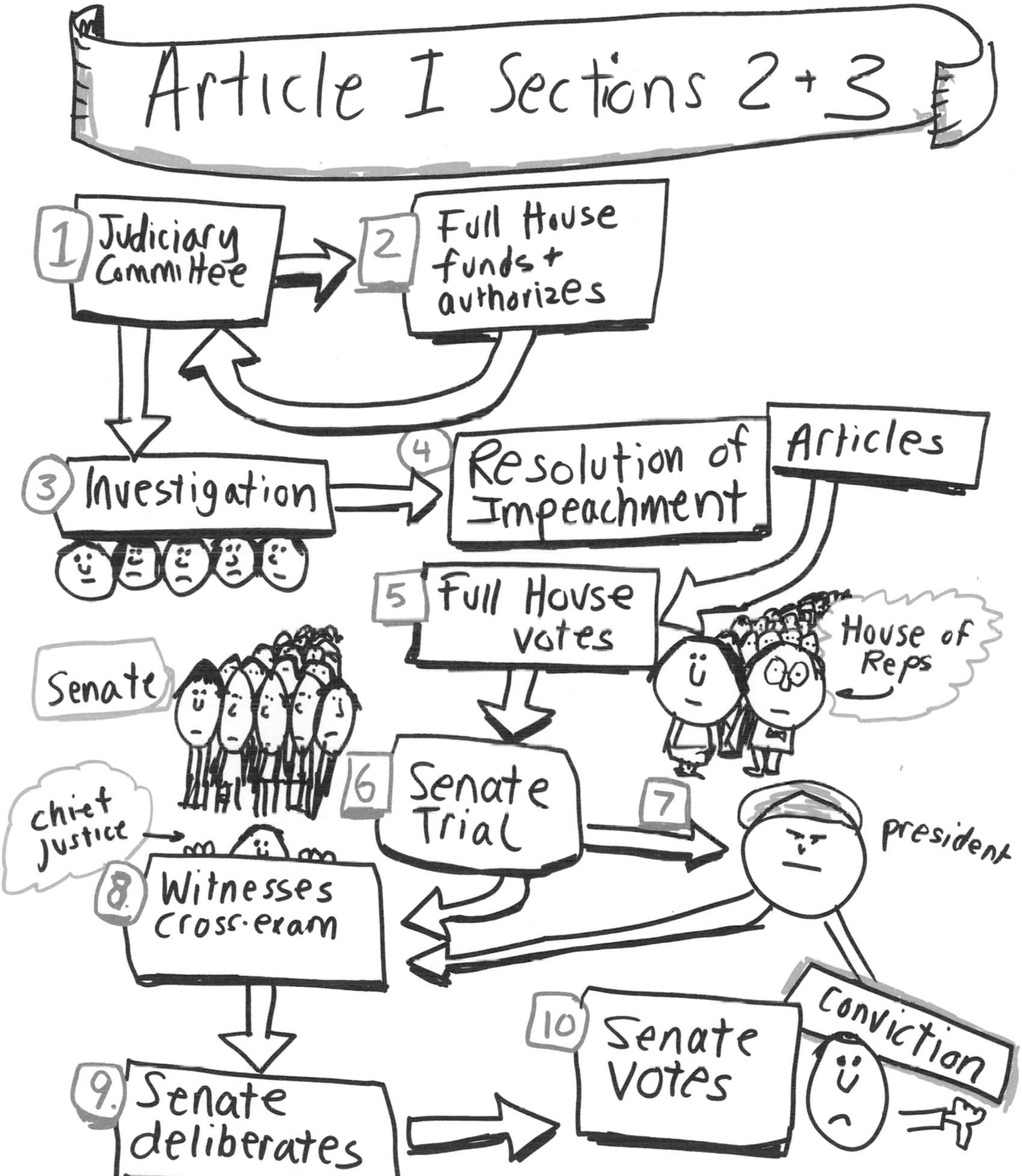

Article I Sections 2 + 3
1 Judiciary Committee
2 Full House funds + authorizes
3 Investigation
4 Resolution of Impeachment
Articles
5 Full House votes
House of Reps
Senate
6 Senate Trial
7
president
chief justice
8 Witnesses cross-exam
9. Senate deliberates
10 Senate Votes
Conviction

FOUR (AND MAYBE FIVE) GROUNDS TO IMPEACH TRUMP

By my count, there are now four grounds to impeach Donald Trump. The fifth appears to be on its way.

FIRST, IN TAKING THE OATH OF OFFICE, A PRESIDENT PROMISES to "faithfully execute the laws and the constitution." That's Article II Section 2.

But Trump is unfaithfully executing his duties as president by accusing his predecessor, President Obama, of undertaking an illegal and impeachable act, with absolutely no evidence to support the accusation.

SECOND, ARTICLE I SECTION 9 OF THE CONSTITUTION FORBIDS GOVERNMENT OFFICIALS from taking things of value from foreign governments. But Trump is making big money off his Trump International Hotel by steering foreign diplomatic delegations to it, and he will make a bundle off China's recent decision to grant his trademark applications for the Trump brand — decisions Chinese authorities arrived at directly because of decisions Trump has made as president.

THIRD, THE FIRST AMENDMENT TO THE CONSTITUTION BARS ANY LAW "RESPECTING AN ESTABLISHMENT OF RELIGION OR PROHIBITING THE FREE EXERCISE THEREOF." But Trump's ban on travel into the United States from six Muslim countries — which he initiated, advocated for, and oversees — violates that provision.

FOURTH, THE FIRST AMENDMENT ALSO BARS "ABRIDGING THE FREEDOM OF THE PRESS." But Trump's labeling the press "the enemy of the people," and choosing who he invites to news conferences based on whether they've given him favorable coverage, violates this provision.

A FIFTH POSSIBLE GROUND, IF THE EVIDENCE IS THERE: Article III Section 3 of the Constitution defines "treason against the United States" as "adhering to their enemies, giving them aid and comfort."

Evidence is mounting that Trump and his aides colluded with Russian operatives to win the 2016 presidential election.

Presidents can be impeached for what the Constitution calls "high crimes and misdemeanors." The question is no longer whether there are grounds to impeach Trump. The practical question is whether there's the political will.

As long as Republicans remain in the majority in the House, where a bill of impeachment originates, it's unlikely. §

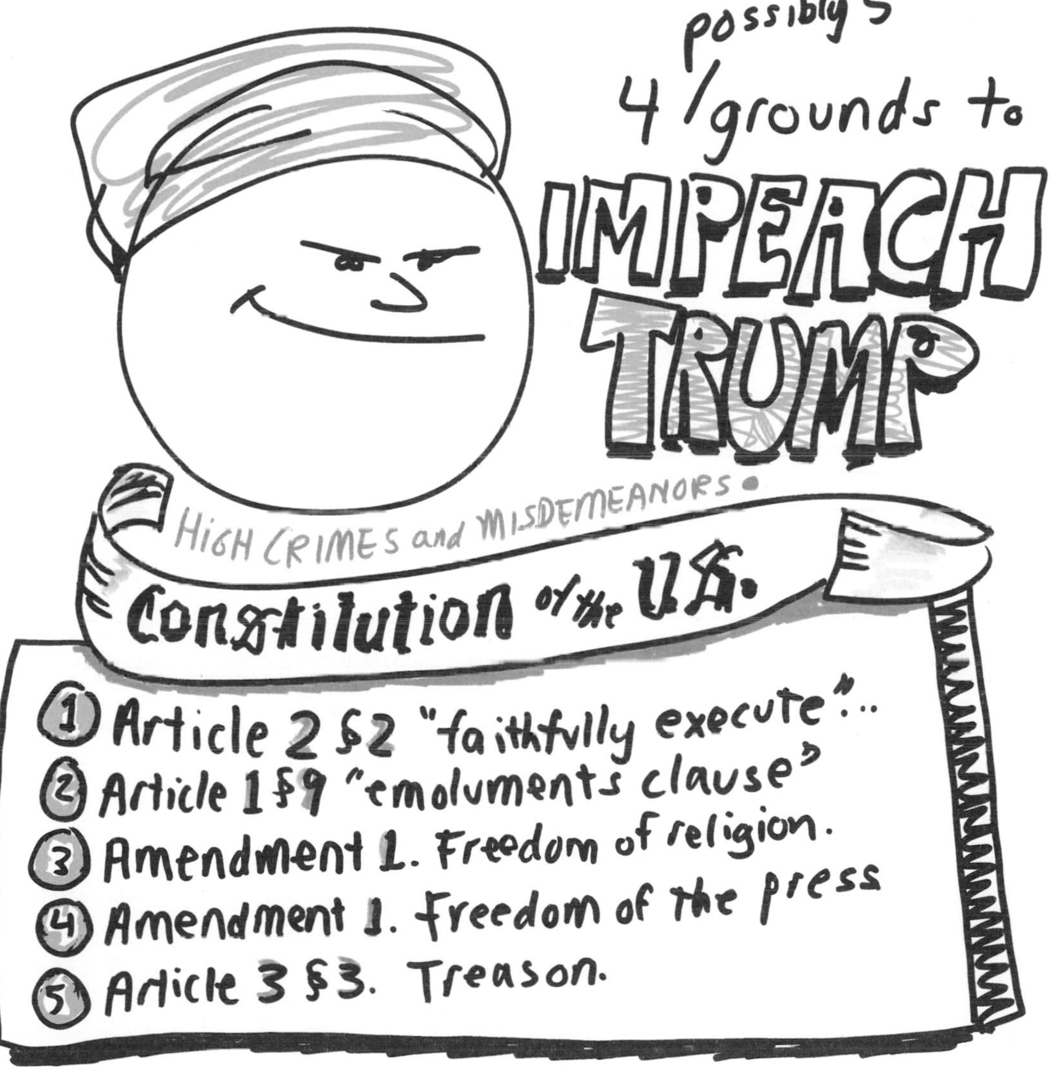
possibly 5
4 grounds to
IMPEACH
TRUMP
HIGH CRIMES and MISDEMEANORS.
Constitution of the U.S.
1 Article 2 §2 "faithfully execute"...
2 Article 1 §9 "emoluments clause"
3 Amendment 1. Freedom of religion.
4 Amendment 1. Freedom of the press
5 Article 3 §3. Treason.

GLOSSARY

American Legislative Exchange Council (ALEC)
A nonprofit organization that drafts legislation for conservative state lawmakers. It is widely considered to be heavily influenced by corporate interests. Its motto is "Limited Government, Free Markets, Federalism."

Antitrust Laws Various U.S. laws designed to promote fair competition among corporations within their industries. These laws primarily prevent price fixing and monopolies.

Big (Ag, Cable, Energy, Money, Oil, Pharma)
The biggest corporations of a certain industry that have the power to lobby the U.S. government to craft laws that provide them with tax and legal preferences and advantages not generally available to small companies within their industry.

Citizens United Shorthand for the 2010 Supreme Court ruling, *Citizens United v. Federal Election Commission*, that allowed corporations and labor unions to spend unlimited sums of money to advocate for or against political candidates.

Debt Ceiling The limit to the amount of money the U.S. can borrow. Congress has always raised the debt ceiling before the U.S. has reached the limit.

Dodd-Frank Act A federal law (formally the Dodd-Frank Wall Street Reform and Consumer Protection Act) intended to regulate the financial industry and thereby prevent a repeat of the conditions that caused the Great Recession of the late 2000s.

Earned Income Tax Credit Federal subsidies that support low- and moderate-income working parents. Families with three or more children receive the most credit, and workers without children receive very little credit.

GDP The total value of all goods and services generated within a country. GDP comprises consumer spending, business investment, government spending, and the value of exports minus imports.

Gerrymandering A practice whereby politicians redraw the boundaries of an electoral district to provide a political advantage to a particular party.

The Great Recession The period from December 2007 to June 2009 when the 8-trillion-dollar housing bubble burst, triggering massive job loss across the U.S.

Mandatory Minimums Sentencing laws that require prison terms of a required length of time for people convicted of certain crimes, especially drug-related offenses, regardless of the circumstances of the offense.

Medicare, Medicaid, ACA, Obamacare   Medicare is a federal health insurance policy available to U.S. citizens aged 65 and over. Medicaid is a healthcare program, federally funded and state run, that assists low-income families with medical costs. The Affordable Care Act, a.k.a. Obamacare, restructured the U.S. healthcare and healthcare insurance system and expanded federal funding and eligibility for Medicaid.

Securities and Exchange Commission   The federal agency in charge of regulating the securities industry. It was established as a result of the Securities Act of 1934, in response to the stock market crash of 1929.

The Sequester   A series of annual spending cuts to federal programs, totaling roughly $1.2 trillion between 2013 and 2021. The 2011 Budget Control Act raised the debt ceiling, but in return for helping to pass the legislation, Republicans demanded spending cuts. The bipartisan committee tasked to plan the cuts failed to reach an agreement, which triggered automatic annual spending cuts.

Speaker of the House   The head of the House of Representatives. He or she has a variety of administrative responsibilities, including administering the oath of office to House members, calling the House to order, preserving order and decorum within the House, and recognizing members to speak on the House floor. The Speaker usually pursues a specific policy agenda.

Superdelegates   During the Democratic Party's presidential primary, voters select delegates to support their preferred candidate in the Democratic National Convention. Superdelegates, however, are party insiders who are free to vote for any candidate they choose.

Tax Havens/Shelters   Tax havens are countries where corporations and wealthy persons bank money to avoid paying taxes, whereas tax shelters are investment strategies that lessen a company or individual's tax burden.

Universal Basic Income   A sum of money sufficient for one to live on given by the government to all its citizens, regardless of income or work status.

U.S. Chamber of Commerce   An American lobbying group (the largest in the U.S.) that supports pro-business causes. It has recently shifted far to the right and has taken extremely conservative positions on issues like climate change and healthcare reform.

Wealth Inequality vs. Income Inequality
Two distinct ways of measuring economic inequality. Income inequality focuses on the disparity between the amounts of money different households make in a given year. Wealth inequality focuses on the disparity between the net worth of different households.

ROBERT B. REICH is Chancellor's Professor of Public Policy at the University of California at Berkeley and Senior Fellow at the Blum Center for Developing Economies. He served as Secretary of Labor in the Clinton administration. He has written the best sellers *Aftershock*, *The Work of Nations*, *Beyond Outrage*, and his most recent, *Saving Capitalism*. He is also a founding editor of *American Prospect* magazine, chairman of Common Cause, a member of the American Academy of Arts and Sciences, and co-creator of the award-winning documentary, *Inequality for All*.